NORTHUMBERLAND & DURHA
LAST DAYS of COLLIERY STE

by

Tom Heavyside

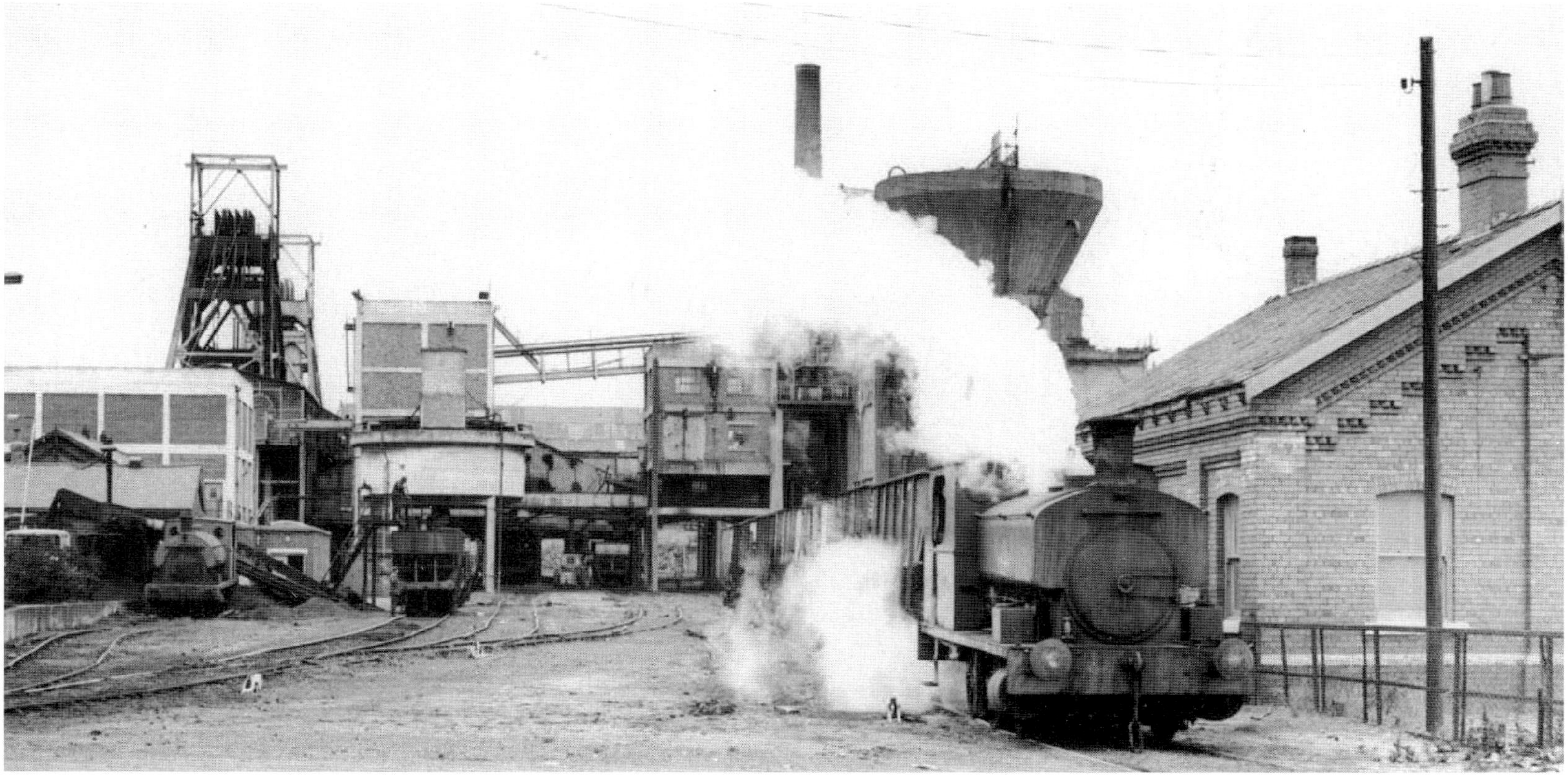

At the start of the 1970s there were still a few engines based in the coalfields of North East England that had originated from outside the area during the early years of the twentieth century, for example these two veterans seen here at Shotton Colliery in County Durham on 29 August 1972. Both 0-6-0STs, the locomotive on the right was manufactured by Andrew Barclay's of Kilmarnock in 1904 (works No. 1015), while that on the left was built by Peckett's of Bristol in 1914 (works No. 1310).

First published in the United Kingdom, 2009,
by Stenlake Publishing Ltd.
www.stenlake.co.uk
ISBN 9781840334616

ACKNOWLEDGEMENTS

While completing this volume I have been grateful for advice and assistance received from Paul Abell, Geoff Creese, Bob Darvill, John Fozard, Roger Hateley, Colin Mountford and the staff of Wigan Heritage Service. My sincere thanks to all.

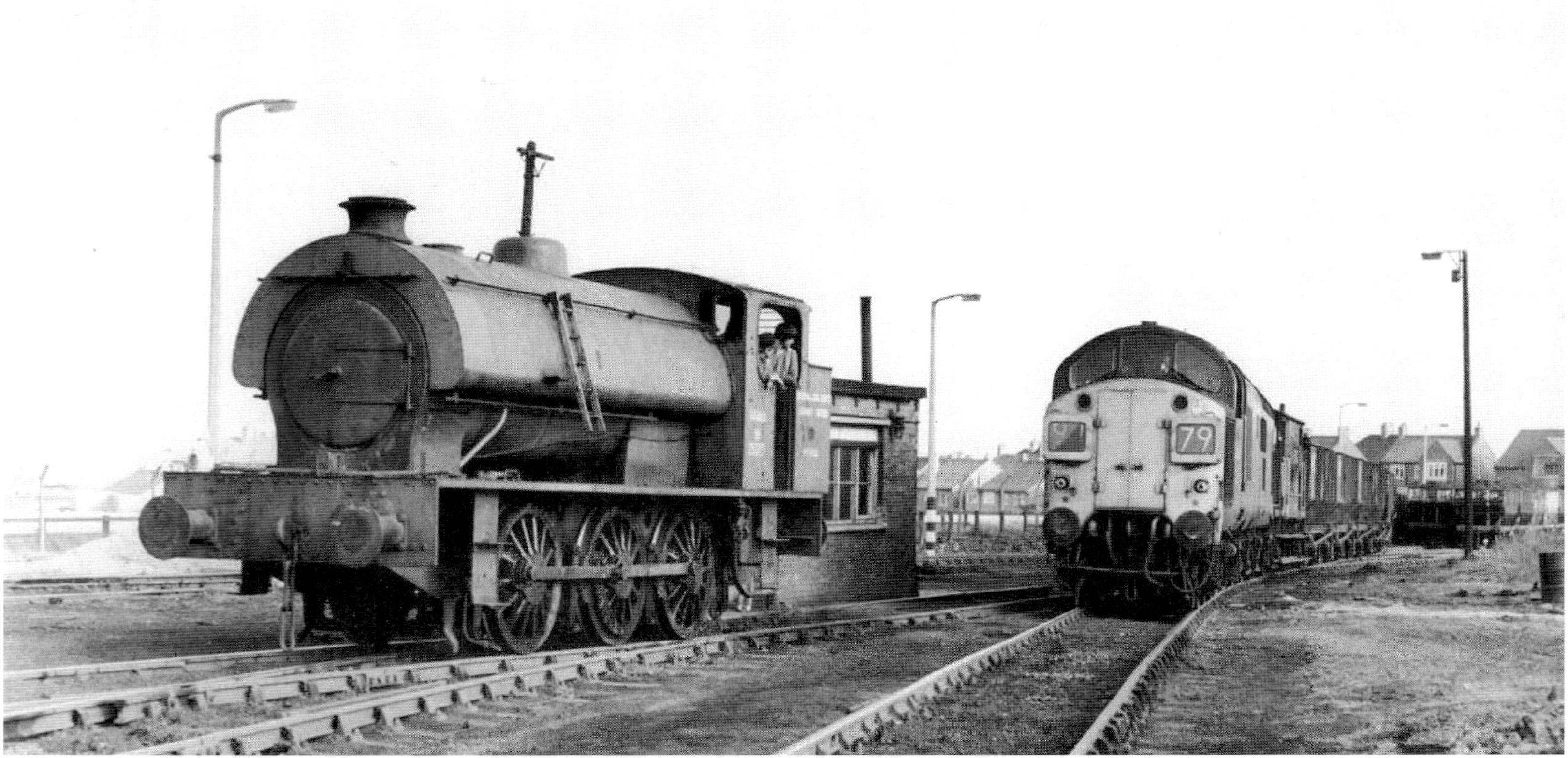

British Railways finally dispensed with steam traction in the North East in September 1967, although for a number of years the replacement diesel locomotives continued to rub shoulders with their steam counterparts at a number of industrial locations. This meeting of old and new took place at Vane Tempest Colliery, Seaham, near the Durham coastline, on 28 August 1974. English Electric 1962-built Class 37 No. 37045 (originally No. D6745) cautiously makes its way back towards the main line, whilst the crew of the colliery shunter, Bagnall 'Austerity' 0-6-0ST works No. 2779, 'Gamma', built in 1945, look on.

INTRODUCTION

The North East of England is often referred to as 'the cradle of the railways', for while the wooden waggonway put down in 1604 between Strelley and Wollaton, near Nottingham, is generally recognised as being the first of its kind, it was the coal-owners of Northumberland and Durham who made the most of the concept during the ensuing years of the seventeenth and eighteenth centuries. The main purpose of these primitive railways was to convey the output from some of the burgeoning mines in the two counties to the Tyne and Wear rivers, from where it was shipped south to London and elsewhere. The motive power in those days was provided by men and horses, assisted where possible by ropes and gravity. Similarly, while the steam locomotive was not born in the North East, some of the local colliery engineers, such as George Stephenson, William Hedley and Timothy Hackworth, played a significant role in its subsequent development during the early years of the nineteenth century.

Later, from the mid 1800s, the rapid expansion of the main line railway network along with improved shipping methods, enabled the heavy and bulky black diamonds to become more widely available, and as a result coal mining and its ancillary activities quickly became the dominant industry in many parts of Northumberland and Durham. While the industry was long past its peak when it was vested in the state at the beginning of 1947, the region's continuing economic dependence on coal can be gauged by the fact that during the first year of its existence the National Coal Board employed 109,908 men in County Durham, with a grand total of 27,026,000 tons of coal being produced from 130 collieries. North of the River Tyne in Northumberland, the efforts of another 42,160 men at sixty-seven collieries realised 11,680,000 tons that same year.

Listed among the diverse assets handed down by the former North East coal-owners to the newly-formed NCB in January 1947 were over 380 steam locomotives, many thousands of wagons and countless other items of railway equipment. The trackwork consisted of many miles of sidings serving the various pits and coking plants, together with a number of quite lengthy lines linking some of the inland pits to various staithes near the North Sea coast.
Following its takeover of the industry, the NCB embarked on a much-needed investment programme, and as part of the upgrading process ninety-one new steam locomotives were purchased for use in the North East, the final one making its appearance in 1957. Not surprisingly, the main supplier was the Tyneside factory of Robert Stephenson & Hawthorns who invoiced the NCB for fifty-eight locomotives over a period of ten years, with another fifteen coming from Andrew Barclay's of Kilmarnock while fourteen emanated from Leeds - ten built by Hunslet, all 'Austerity' 0-6-0STs, and four by their near neighbours Hudswell Clarke. The remainder comprised three four-wheeled vertical-boilered engines received from Sentinel's of Shrewsbury in 1955 for use at Derwenthaugh Coke Works at Blaydon, and a solitary example from Peckett's of Bristol for which a cheque was issued in 1947, although this had in fact been ordered prior to nationalisation by Pelaw Main Collieries. A further thirty-four locomotives were acquired second-hand from various sources, the last a former British Railways-owned 'Austerity' No. 68050, bought as a source of spares in 1965. In addition a few engines were obtained from other NCB areas, including three 'Austerities' which arrived at Ashington in 1965 after being made redundant by the NCB East Midlands Division Area No. 5 (Ilkeston). During this period many older, worn-out locomotives were sold to the scrap metal industry.

At the turn of the decade into the 1970s, due to colliery closures and an influx of diesel locomotives, the number of steam engines owned by the NCB in the two counties had gradually been reduced to 104, these being the products of eleven different private locomotive works. The fleet consisted of seventy-seven with an 0-6-0 wheel arrangement, sixty-six of which were fitted with a saddle tank, ten with side tanks and one with a pannier tank, along with twenty-three 0-4-0STs and four 0-6-2Ts. They were dispersed between thirty-three locations.

However, during the early 1970s the dependence on steam power fell sharply, and as of 1 January 1976 only nineteen engines, made up of fifteen 0-6-0STs (including eleven 'Austerities'), three 0-4-0STs and one 0-6-0T, remained on the books of the NCB in the North East. By the mid 1970s there was very little steam activity in the area, only four engines surviving into the 1980s and they too were soon discarded. In effect the end of steam also foreshadowed the end of coal mining in the two counties, for within a quarter of a century the last deep mine had been closed. The conclusion came about rather abruptly in

January 2005 when, following some flooding problems, UK Coal Mining Ltd abandoned Ellington Colliery, near Ashington.

Today the landscape of the coalfields has been radically altered from the sight that greeted visitors in the past, for no longer do the headstocks of numerous pits rise majestically above their surroundings, the staithes have been dismantled (except at Dunston on the south bank of the Tyne) and the railway tracks that served them mostly torn up, all of no use in the present age. In its wake regeneration has brought much cleaner industries and even the coastline is now virtually as nature intended since it is no longer continually contaminated by colliery waste and particles of coal.

Nevertheless the once-proud coal industry has not been forgotten. For instance at the former Woodhorn Colliery, near Ashington, an impressive visitor centre has recently been created, honouring many former aspects of Northumberland life, including the part played by coal. Similarly, at the North of England Open Air Museum at Beamish in County Durham the coal mine and its associated buildings are prominent features at this recreated village. In addition a number of local monuments have been erected in recent years as tangible reminders of some of the extinct collieries, often incorporating a pulley wheel.

On the railway front, in County Durham the Tanfield Railway hosts a splendid collection of mainly ex-colliery locomotives, some gathered from afar, at their Marley Hill engine shed headquarters. The shed originally belonged to the Pontop & Jarrow Railway (later the Bowes Railway) while nearer the coast, along the path of this former dedicated coal-carrying railway, is the smaller but equally important Bowes Railway Centre at Springwell. On the other side of the Tyne in Northumberland the Stephenson Railway Museum at Middle Engine Lane, near Chirton, utilises a section of the ex-Backworth Colliery Railway as a demonstration line. As for the NCB locomotives that survived into the 1970s in the North East, no less than thirty-one have been preserved, including a number that have been moved to new homes in other parts of Britain. Many people, like the author, have fond memories of visits to various collieries in Northumberland and Durham and the railways that served them, and it is indeed appropriate that they continue to be commemorated and their remnants preserved.

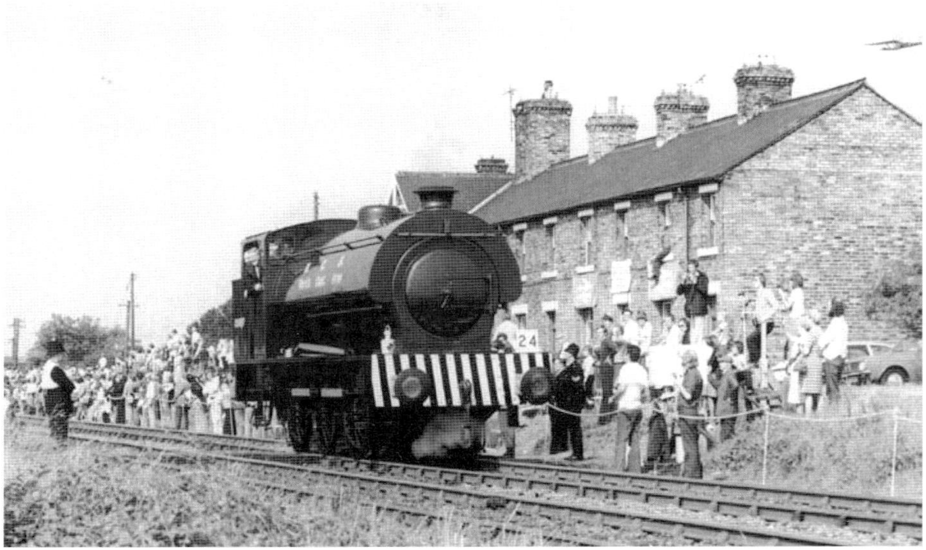

During the last week of August 1975, British Railways staged an exhibition of locomotives and rolling stock at Shildon Wagon Works to commemorate the 150th anniversary of the opening of the Stockton & Darlington Railway in 1825. Rightfully taking its place alongside some elite motive power was the Bagnall 'Austerity' 0-6-0ST, 'Gamma', normally based at Vane Tempest Colliery, Seaham (see pages 2 and 34 to 37). The celebrations culminated in a grand cavalcade of the exhibits from Shildon to Darlington on Sunday 31 August, when thousands of people massed by the lineside to enjoy the spectacle. Here, suitably resplendent for the occasion, 'Gamma' passes Heighington on its way to Darlington. In the procession it was immediately preceded by the replica 'Locomotion', outwardly constructed to the design of its namesake of 1825 specially for the event, and followed by Stanier 'Black 5' 4-6-0 No. 4767 'George Stephenson'.

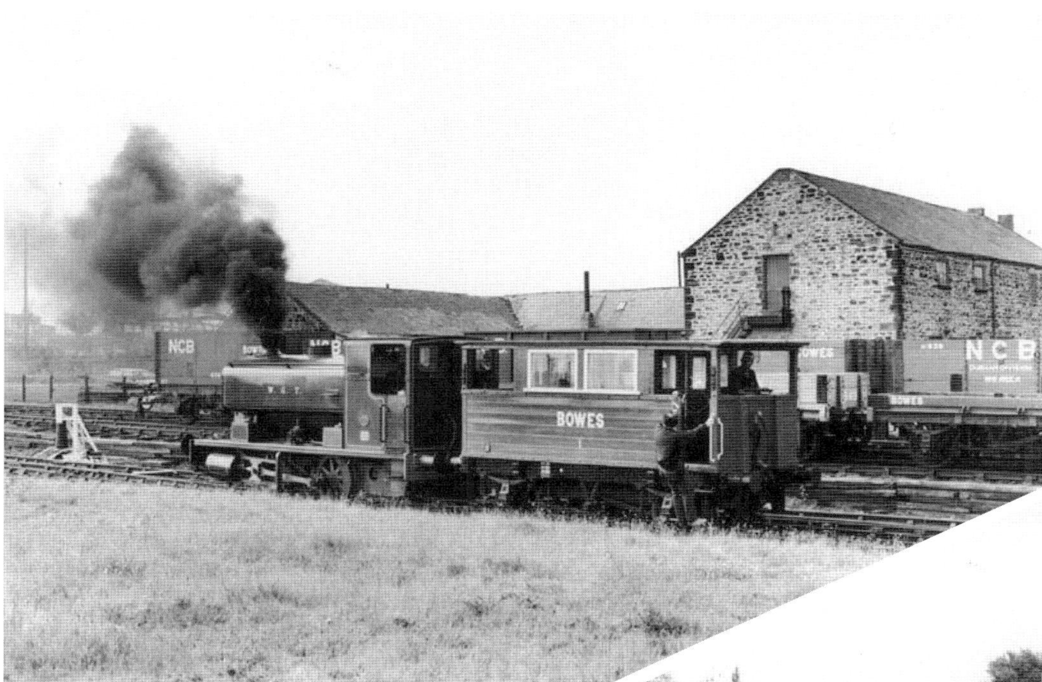

The Bowes Railway Centre at Springwell, between Gateshead and Washington, makes use of what were once the engineering and wagon shops of the erstwhile Bowes Railway (formerly Pontop & Jarrow). Here, Andrew Barclay 0-4-0ST works No. 2361, 'W.S.T.', built in 1954 and previously owned by British Gypsum, shunts a brake van on 27 May 1990. The latter was built for the coal-carrying Lambton Railway at their workshops in Philadelphia, County Durham. Behind are just a small selection of the wagons to be found here, while the upper floor of the building on the right, formerly the joiners' shop, is now used as an exhibition hall. The site includes a couple of rope-worked inclines and these and their attendant engine house have been designated a Scheduled Ancient Monument.

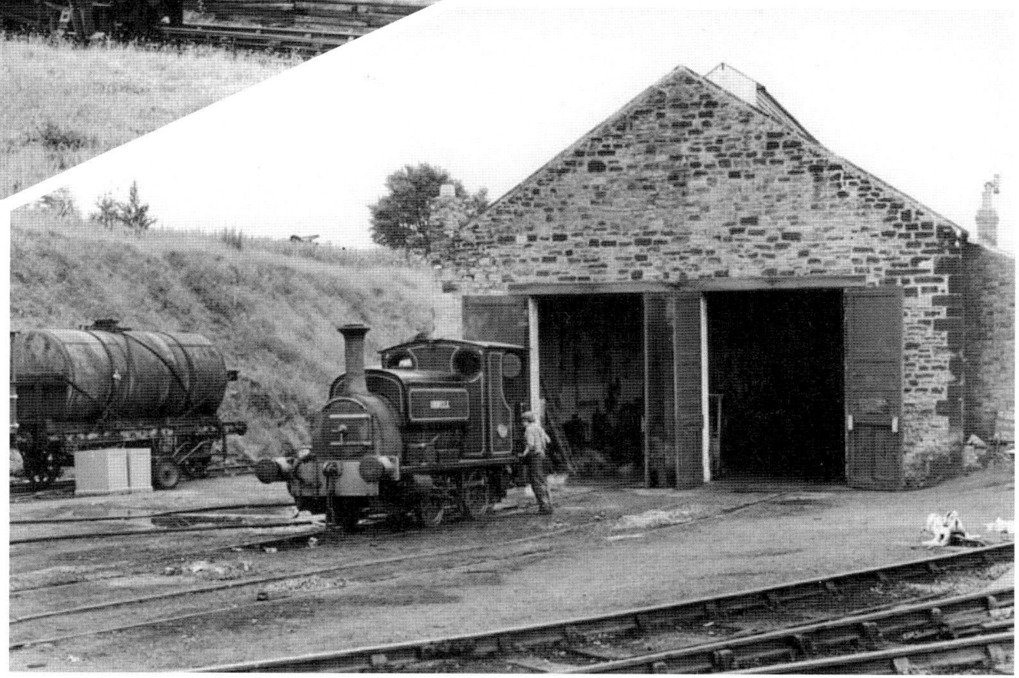

At its peak the Bowes Railway, including six rope-operated inclines, stretched fifteen miles or so inland from the staithes at Jarrow. The two-road, stone-built engine shed at Marley Hill, dating back to the mid 1850s, served the western end of the railway until it was finally abandoned by the NCB in 1970. Still fulfilling its intended purpose, it is now the headquarters of the Tanfield Railway. Seen here outside the shed on 31 July 1994 is Hudswell Clarke 0-4-0ST works No. 1672, 'Irwell', built in 1937, a former Central Electricity Generating Board Lancashire-based engine.

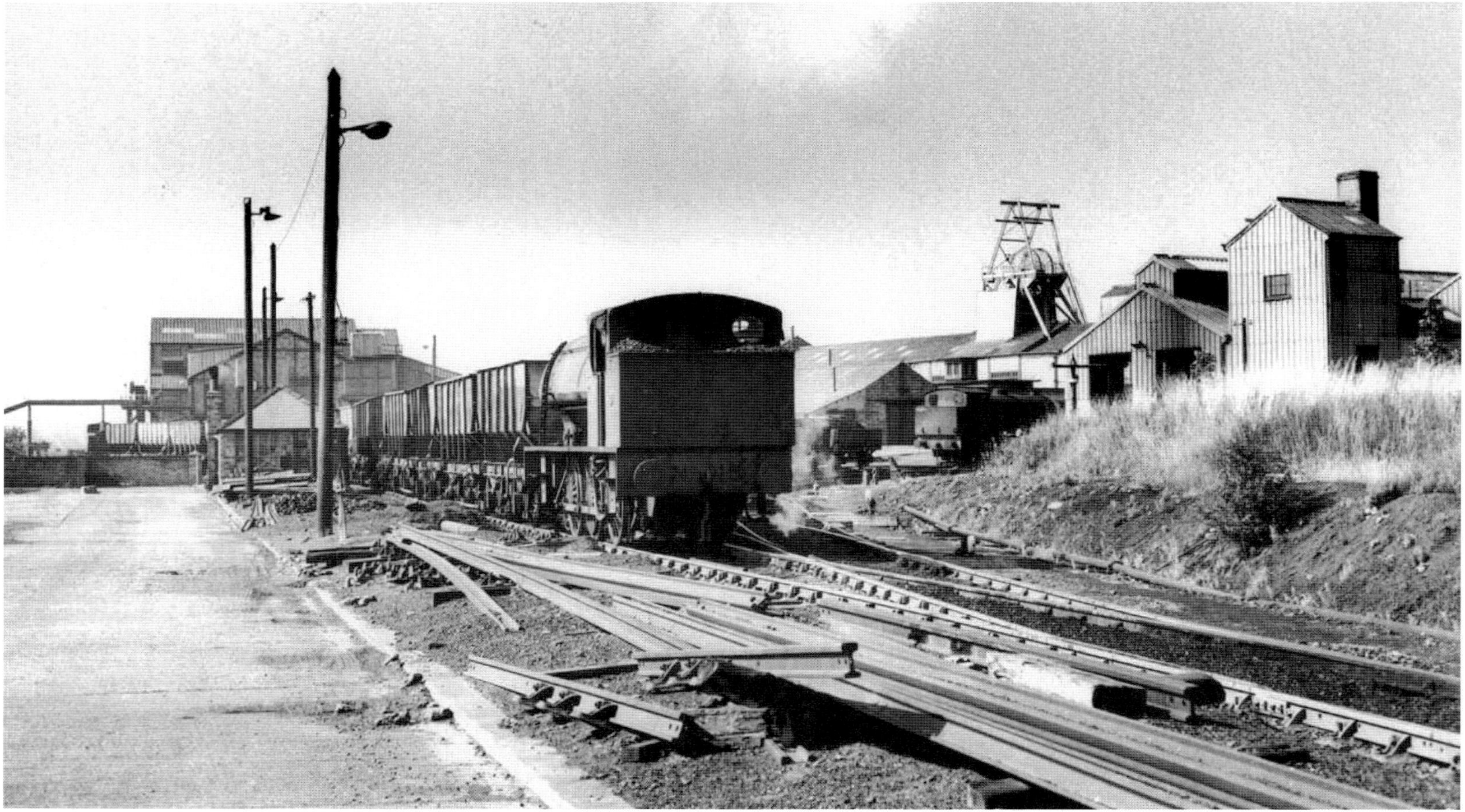

Shilbottle Colliery, situated in a rural setting one mile east of the village of the same name and three miles south-east of the market town of Alnwick, was the NCB's most northerly outlet in Northumberland. The mine was developed by the Co-operative Wholesale Society after they had taken it over in 1917 from what had previously been a small concern owned by the Shilbottle Coal Company. Under the first year of state ownership in 1947, the pit despatched approximately 100,000 tons of high quality coal for domestic, steam and gas purposes, with 540 men being dependent on the mine for their weekly wages. By 1962 productivity was much higher, for while staff numbers had increased to 807, the total output for the year topped 250,000 tons. Shunting a rake of hopper wagons on 31 August 1972, is Robert Stephenson & Hawthorns 'Austerity' 0-6-0ST NCB No. 45, built in 1943 at the company's Forth Banks Works in Newcastle-upon-Tyne (works No. 7113). On the right, outside the two-road, corrugated-iron engine shed, with the winding wheels towering overhead is NCB No. 48, an 'Austerity' put together by the Hunslet Engine Company at their Jack Lane factory, Leeds, in 1944 (works No. 3172).

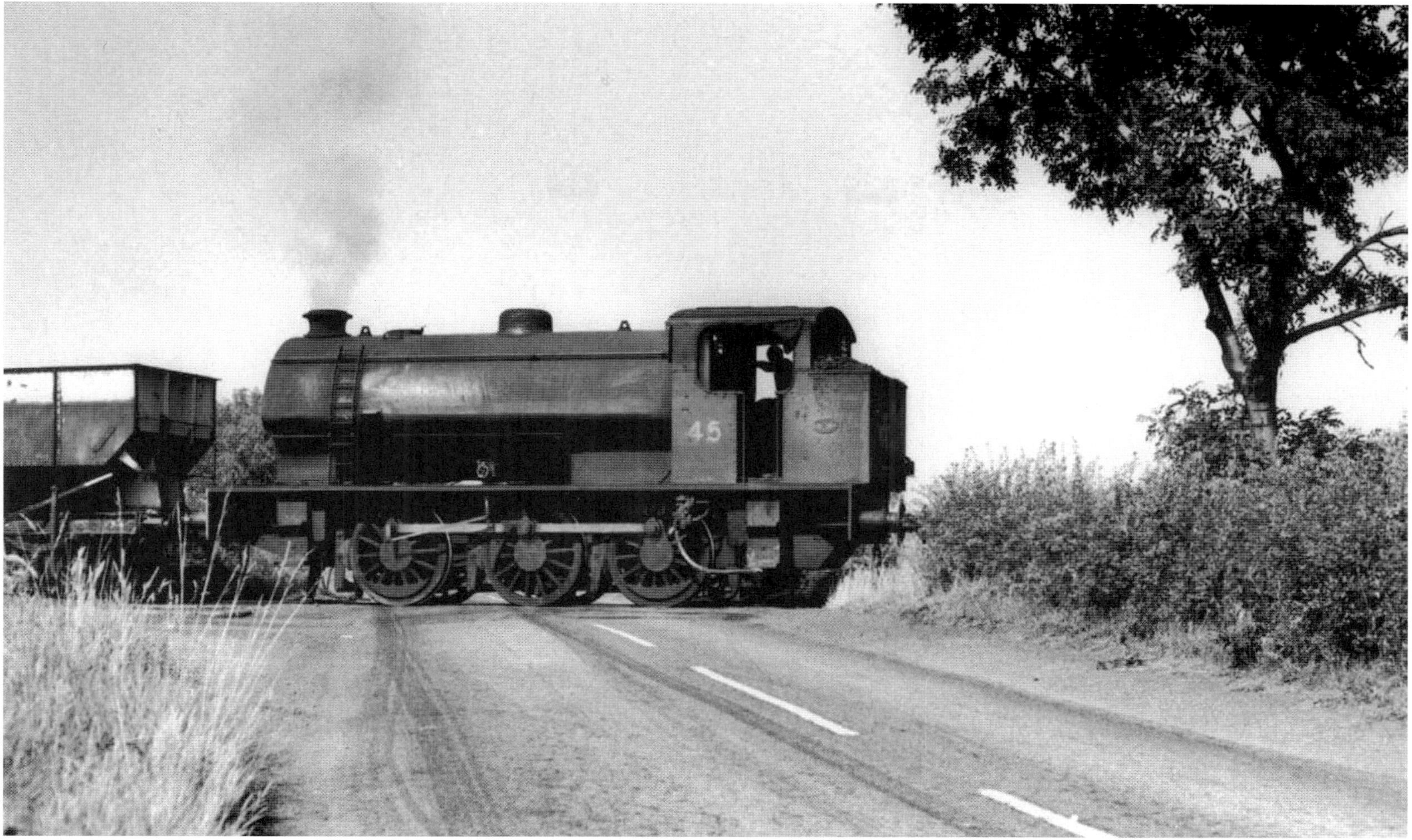

A broadside view of No. 45 on the same day as the previous photograph as it crosses the minor road by the entrance to Shilbottle Colliery. No. 45 had a somewhat varied career. It was delivered new in October 1943 to the Army depot at Burton Dassett, near Kineton, between Banbury and Stratford-upon-Avon, as WD (War Department) No. 75077, one of ninety 'Austerities' ordered by the Ministry of Supply from Robert Stephenson & Hawthorns between 1943 and 1945. Almost immediately it was loaned to the Port of London Authority and then, from April 1944, to the Ministry of Fuel & Power. After being returned to the Port of London Authority sometime during 1945 it was purchased by them in April 1946, when it became PLA No. 86. It was sold to the NCB in October 1960, having spells of duty at Ashington as well as at Shilbottle.

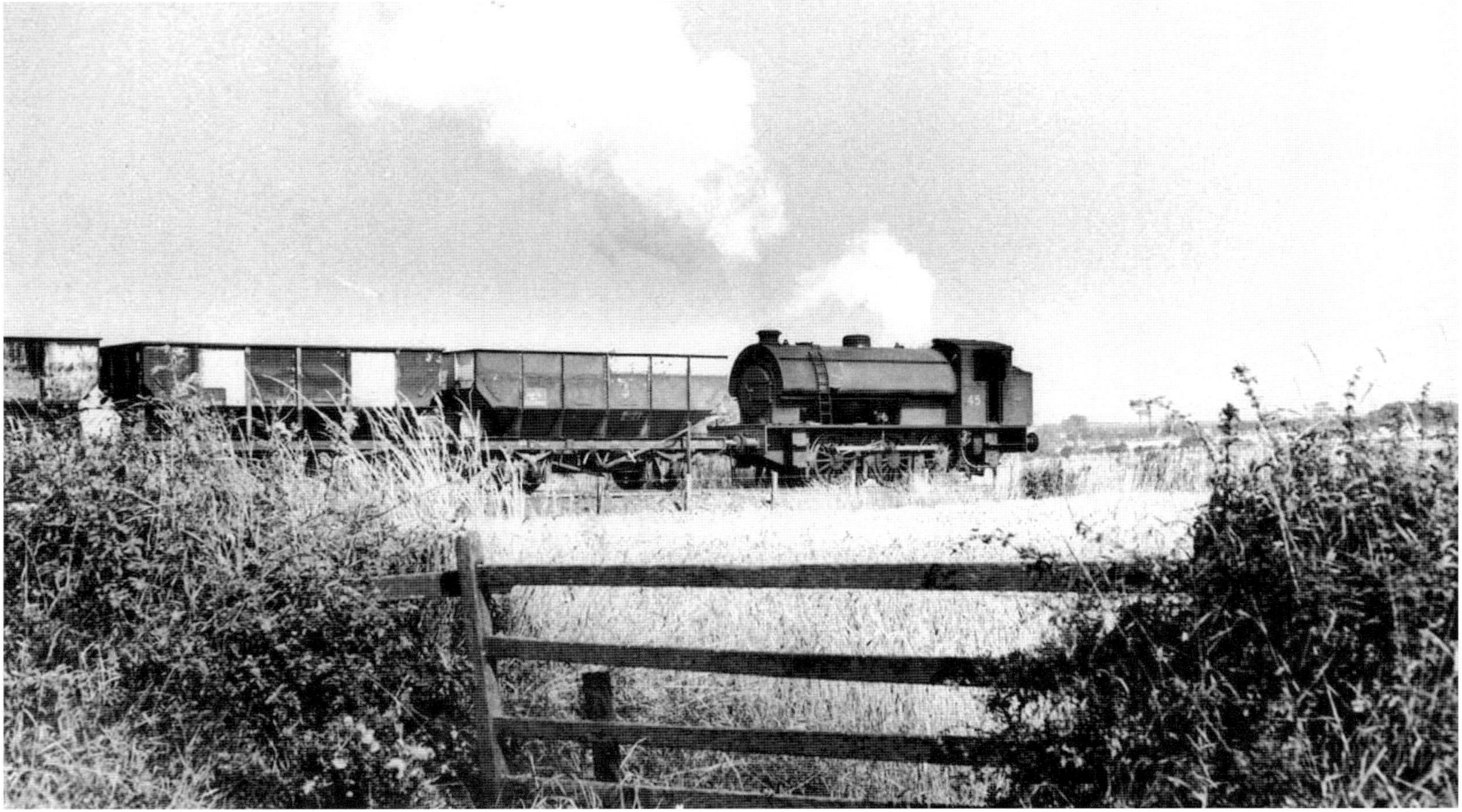

The pastoral surroundings of the colliery at Shilbottle are evident in this photograph of No. 45 as it starts out along the one-and-a-half mile branch to the BR exchange sidings by the East Coast main line, again on 31 August 1972. Rail traffic ended here in February 1978 when the coal was redirected underground to nearby Whittle Colliery, although Shilbottle retained its separate identity until October 1982 when it was officially closed and the staff transferred to Whittle. As regards No. 45, this was scrapped in March 1973. Its sister engine, 'Austerity' No. 48, was a little more fortunate in that it was moved south to Backworth shed the same month, albeit causing the confusing situation of two No. 48s sharing the same accommodation. In fact a similar situation had occurred at Shilbottle a little earlier, with one of the engines involved then rather bizarrely being renumbered 38½ in order to distinguish it from its shed mate! These duplications were due to various NCB area managements adopting their own numbering schemes, subsequent amalgamations and reallocations creating such anomalies.

Whittle Colliery, a drift mine, located four miles south of Alnwick at Newton-on-the-Moor, was very close to the A1 trunk road, although well-camouflaged from passing traffic. Like Shilbottle, it was acquired by the Co-operative Wholesale Society in 1917 when it was just a small landsale outlet, previously having been owned by the South Shilbottle Coal Company. Again, as at Shilbottle, during the mid 1920s the CWS invested heavily in the mine, including the construction of a four-and-a-half mile long railway from the pit yard to Southside, between Acklington and Warkworth, where exchange sidings were constructed by the East Coast main line.

During the early years of the NCB's tenure at Whittle, the pit yielded approximately 60,000 tons of coal per annum from the same seam as that mined by Shilbottle and provided a living for some 270 men. A major development in the mid 1960s saw a new drift driven underground half-a-mile to the south of the original adit, whereupon a conveyor belt carried some 250,000 tons of coal per annum up a 1-in-3 incline to the surface. By that time, over 630 men were collecting their weekly wage packets from the pit offices.

Seen here on 31 August 1972, Robert Stephenson & Hawthorns 0-6-0ST works No. 7849, NCB No. 47, built in October 1955, runs forward from the stabling siding in preparation for its next assignment. The locomotive was originally handed over to the Backworth Colliery Railway as an oil-burner, one of a few that were trialled by the NCB. It remained at Backworth, apart from works visits for repairs and overhauls, until it was moved to Whittle in December 1971, by which time the engine had been converted to burn coal in the conventional manner. It had 17in. diameter outside cylinders with a 24in. stroke and 3ft 10in. diameter wheels. The boiler was pressed to 170lb. per square inch, giving a nominal tractive effort of 21,788lb. when calculated at 85% of maximum boiler pressure.

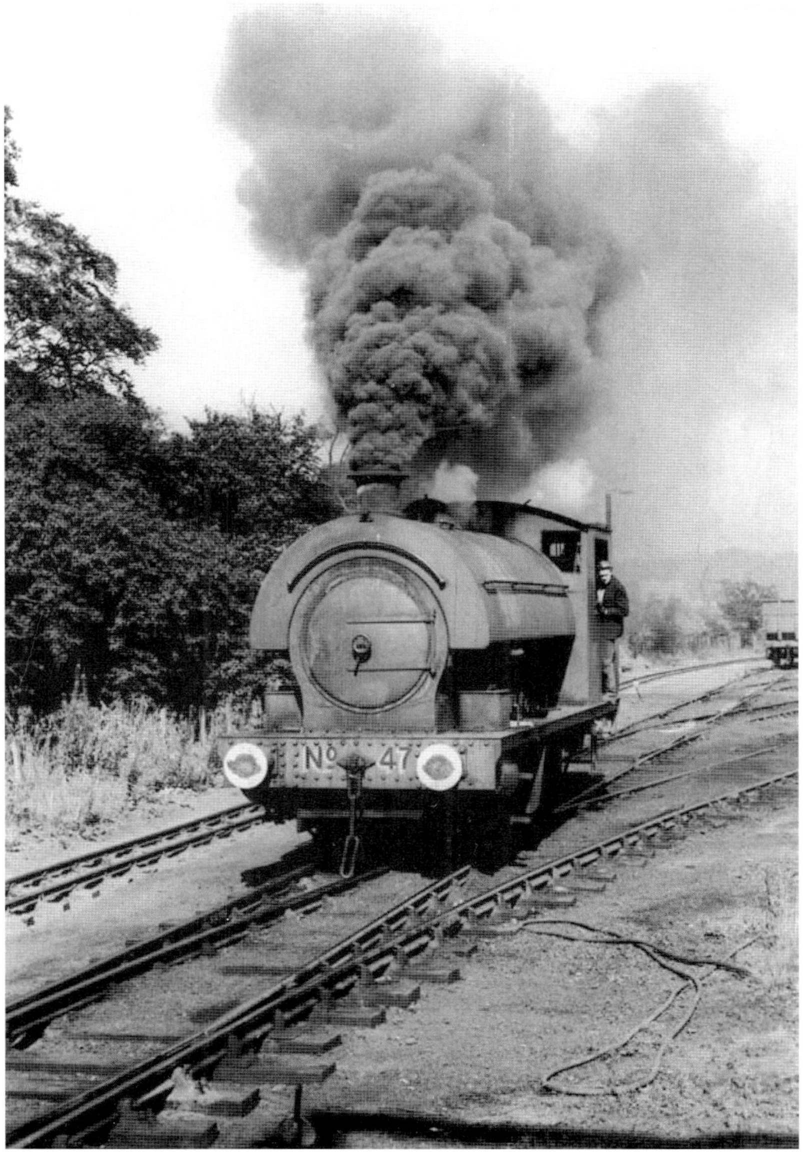

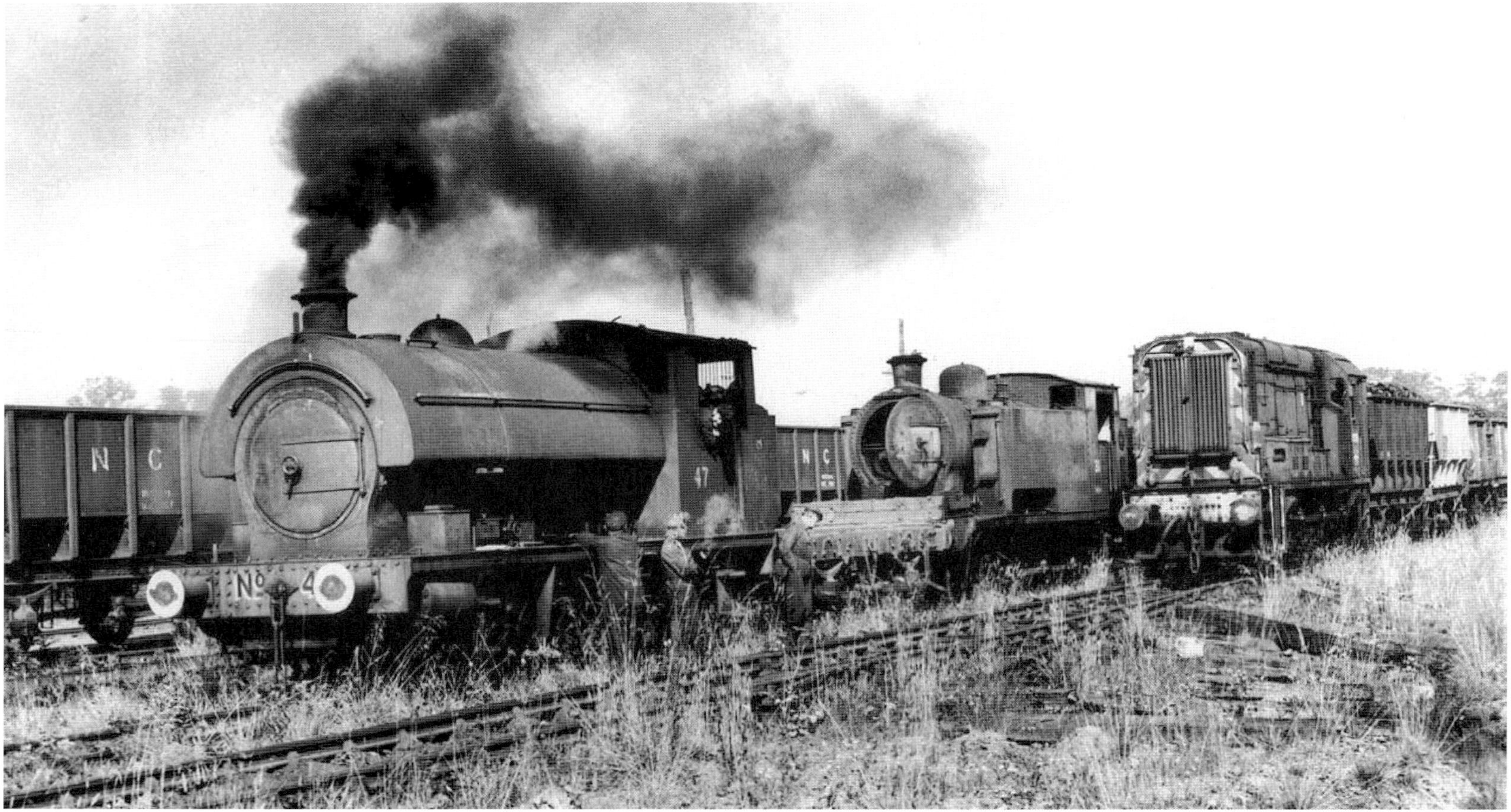

In this photograph, taken on the same day as the previous exposure, standing behind No. 47 in the stabling siding at Whittle (no shed was provided here) is NCB No. 31, one of five side tanks ordered by the NCB from Robert Stephenson & Hawthorns for use on the extensive Ashington system. No. 31 (works No. 7609) was the last of three put together in 1950 with 18in. x 26in. inside cylinders and 4ft 6in. diameter wheels. At 85% of the maximum boiler pressure of 180lb. per square inch the trio could exert a tractive effort of 23,868lb. The other two RSH side tanks, supplied in 1954, differed from their predecessors in that they were equipped with 18in. x 24in. outside cylinders which rendered them slightly less powerful than the earlier examples. No. 31 arrived at Whittle from Ashington in May 1969 and remained there until moved to the fledgling North Yorkshire Moors Railway at Grosmont in March 1973. It is now based on the Avon Valley Railway at Bitton, between Bristol and Bath. Coming into view on the right, beginning the journey to the BR exchange sidings at Southside, is BR Class 08 diesel-electric No. D3215 (later renumbered 08147), which was on hire to the NCB. *En route* the train would negotiate four level crossings, the shunter needing to climb down on each occasion to supervise its passage over these quiet country lanes.

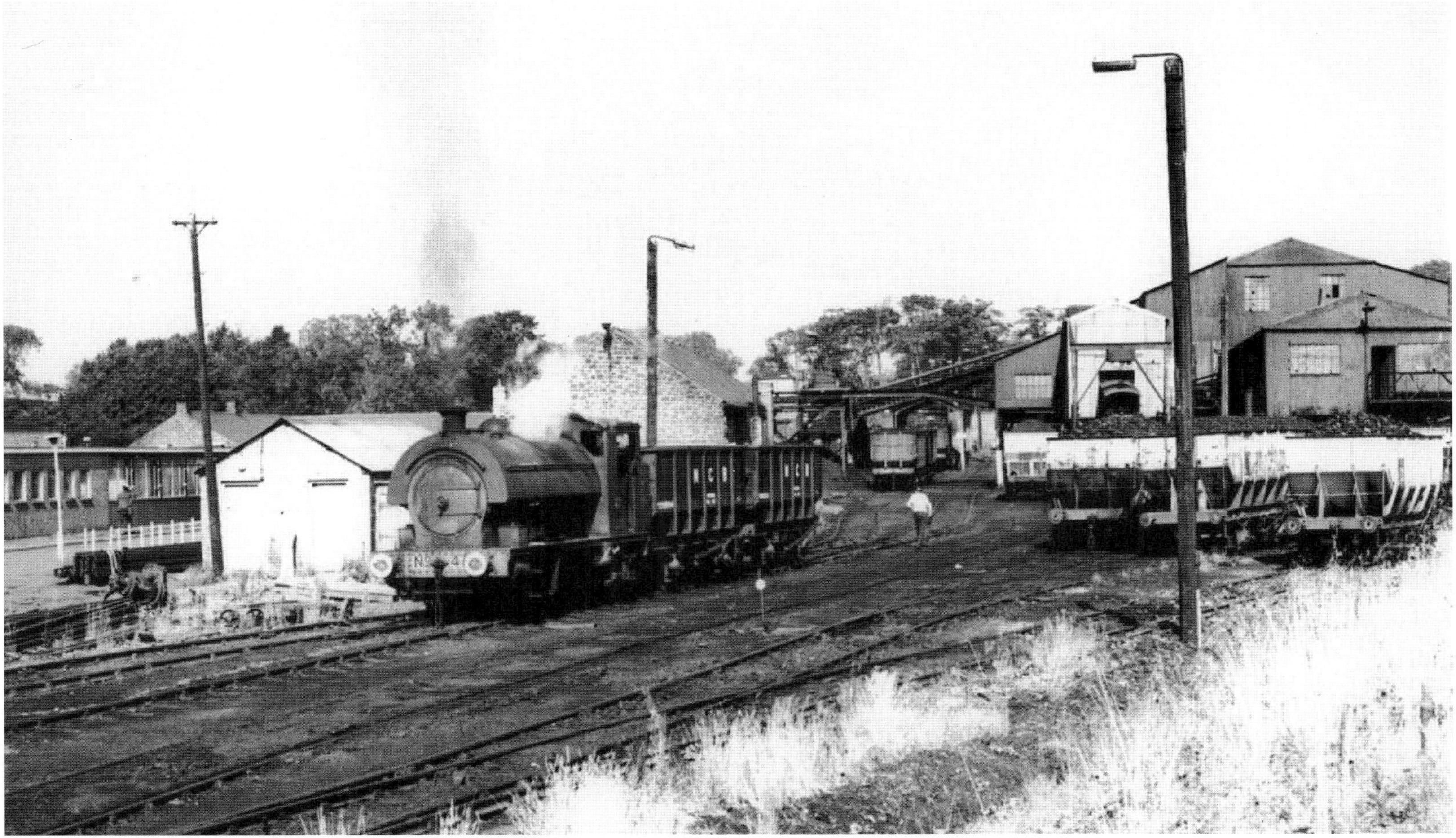

Later on the same day, No. 47 shunts the yard at Whittle. Engaged on what was referred to as 'the short run', one of the engine's tasks was to bring short rakes of 21-ton capacity hopper wagons laden with freshly hewn coal from the mouth of the drift to the yard, where it was screened and washed, before being sold for local use or taken to the BR exchange sidings. The next year, in September 1973, No. 47 followed in the wake of No. 31 to the North Yorkshire Moors Railway, but like its former companion has since moved on to pastures new, having taken up residence on the Lincolnshire Wolds Railway at Ludborough, between Cleethorpes and Louth. Following the departure of the steam locomotives the mine relied on a number of diesels, although after the summer of 1983, when the branch to Southside ('the long run') was last used, only 'the short run' duty remained, pending closure at the beginning of 1987. The mine was later taken over by a private concern, but production ceased for a second and final time in April 1996.

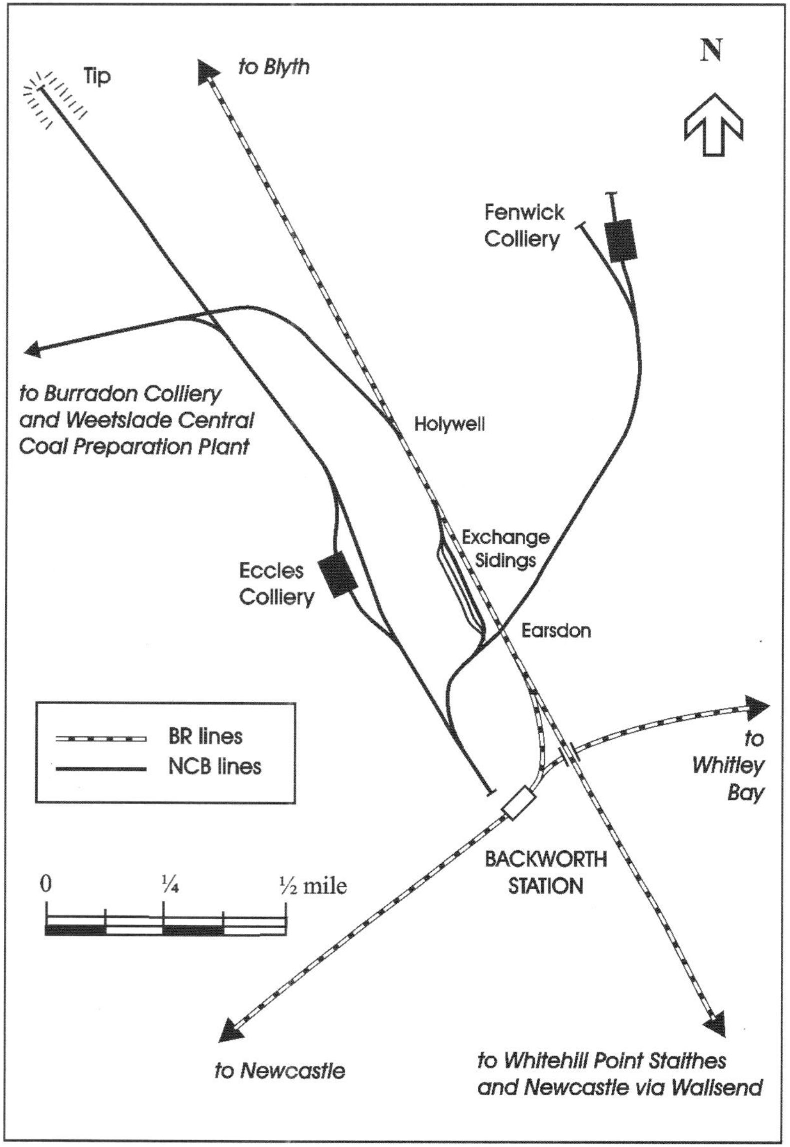

A diagram of the railways in the Backworth area during the early 1970s. The history of the colliery lines can traced back to 1818, when coal was first carried from Backworth 'A' pit, located three miles inland from the shoreline at Whitley Bay, down to Whitehill Point Staithes on the north bank of the River Tyne, a distance of four miles. In fact, two miles of the route had been utilised in earlier times by a wooden waggonway constructed to assist the movement of coal to the staithes from pits sunk at Murton and Shiremoor. Following the completion of Backworth 'A' Colliery, the Backworth Coal Company quickly began to develop other mines in the area and what became known as the Backworth Colliery Railway expanded accordingly.

However, by 1970, of the numerous collieries and an opencast site that had once provided traffic for the railway, only Eccles, near the site of Backworth 'A', and Fenwick collieries remained in production. As a consequence some sections of the railway had already been abandoned, including the line to Whitehill Point which had been severed to the south of Eccles Colliery in August 1969. Noteworthy is the fact that trains serving Fenwick Colliery had to cross over the former Blyth & Tyne Railway (North Eastern Railway from August 1874) on the level by Earsdon signal box, and similarly those delivering stone (waste material) to the tip had to pass over the branch from Holywell to the Burradon Colliery system at Fisher Lane. The tip was on the site of the old Backworth 'C' pit, closed over seventy years earlier in 1895.

In January 1970 seven steam locomotives were allocated to Backworth shed, with up to four being needed in service on most days. During the ensuing years the stock was bolstered by a further three locomotives transferred in from elsewhere, although during the final months of steam only two were required on duty at any one time. By the time the inevitable happened and steam surrendered to diesel power at the end of 1975, Backworth had already entered the history books as the last place in Northumberland to maintain steam in commercial service. Rail operations ceased altogether in July 1980, when clearance work was completed following the closure of Eccles Colliery the previous May.

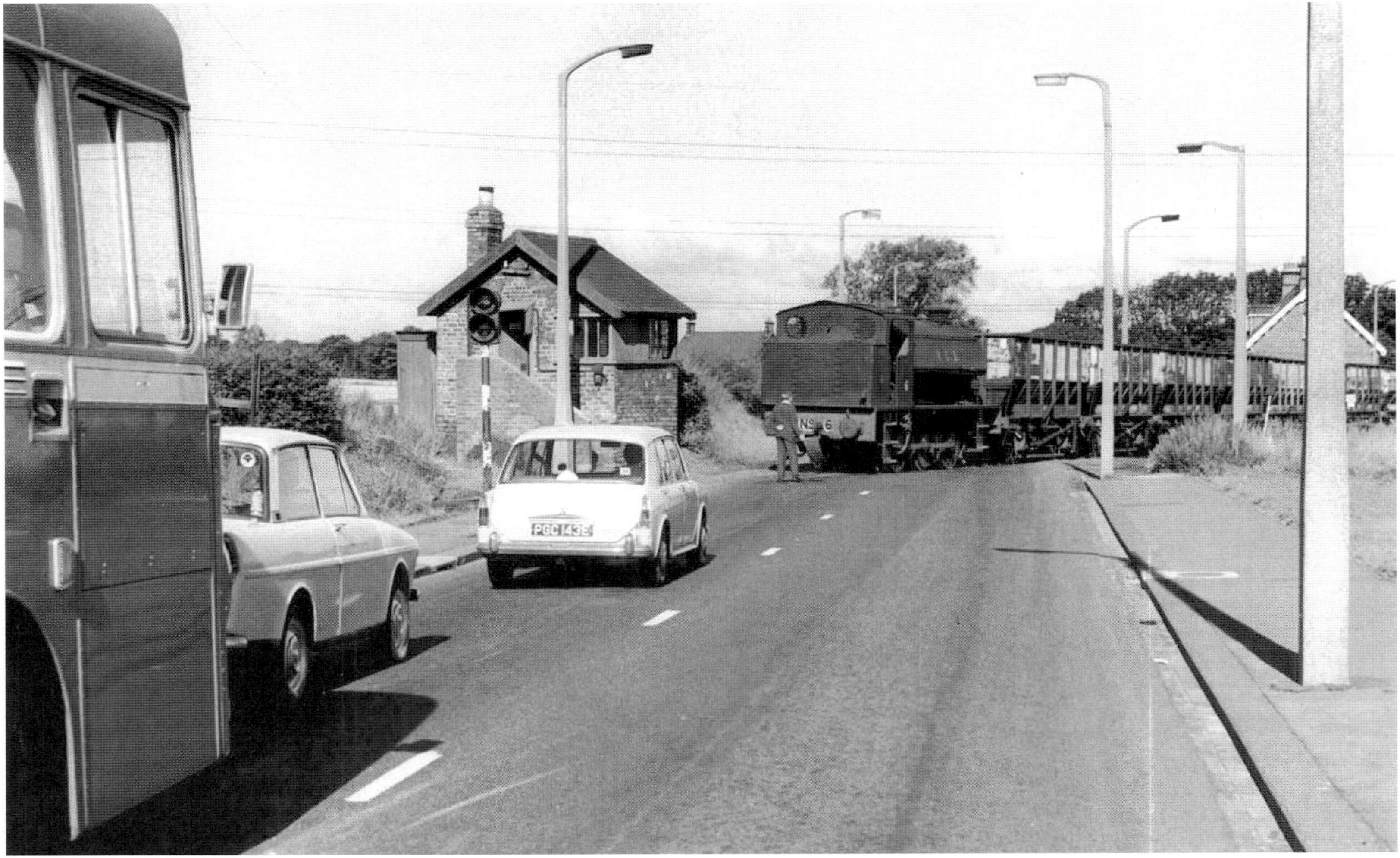

At the south end of Eccles Colliery at Backworth on the morning of 27 August 1974, passengers on a local bus service and the occupants of two cars, a DAF and a 1967-registered Austin, wait patiently while Bagnall 'Austerity' 0-6-0ST works No. 2749, NCB No. 6, built in 1944, propels some empty wagons across the B1322 road towards the pit. Meanwhile, the crossing keeper ensures the safety of all concerned. Just beyond the Austin car is the substantial brick-built cabin from where the simple stop/go traffic signals were operated. Leading out of the frame to the left is the short stub of track retained as a headshunt when the route to the staithes at Whitehill Point was closed in 1969.

BR Class 37 No. 37082 heads north with a solitary brake van in tow along the Blyth & Tyne line, while No. 6 prepares to depart from the exchange sidings with some empty wagons ready for refilling at Eccles Colliery, again on 27 August 1974. The sidings were only commissioned during the late 1960s.

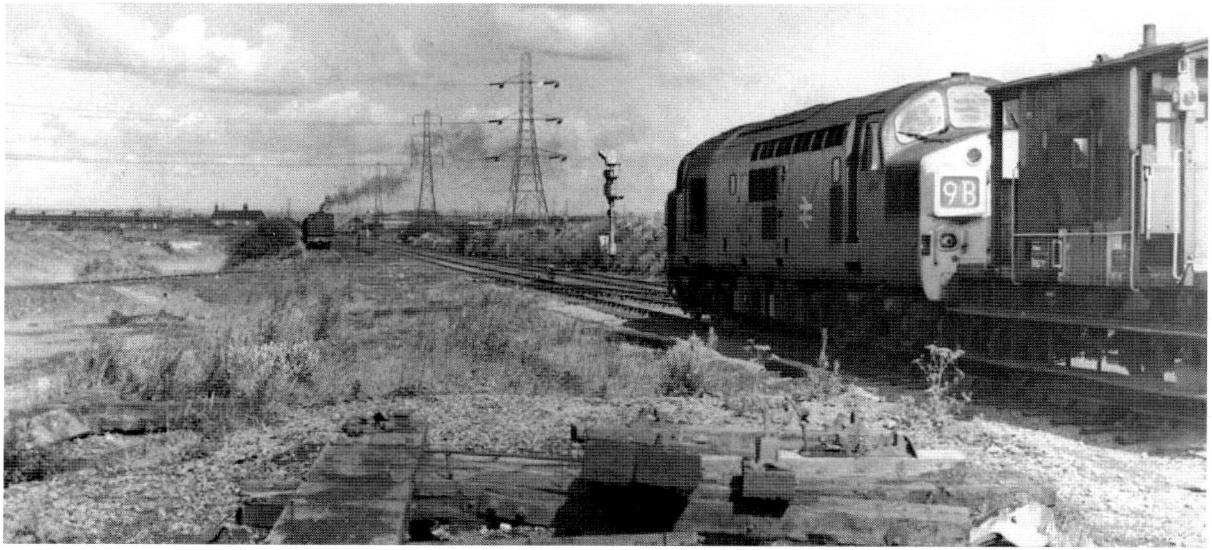

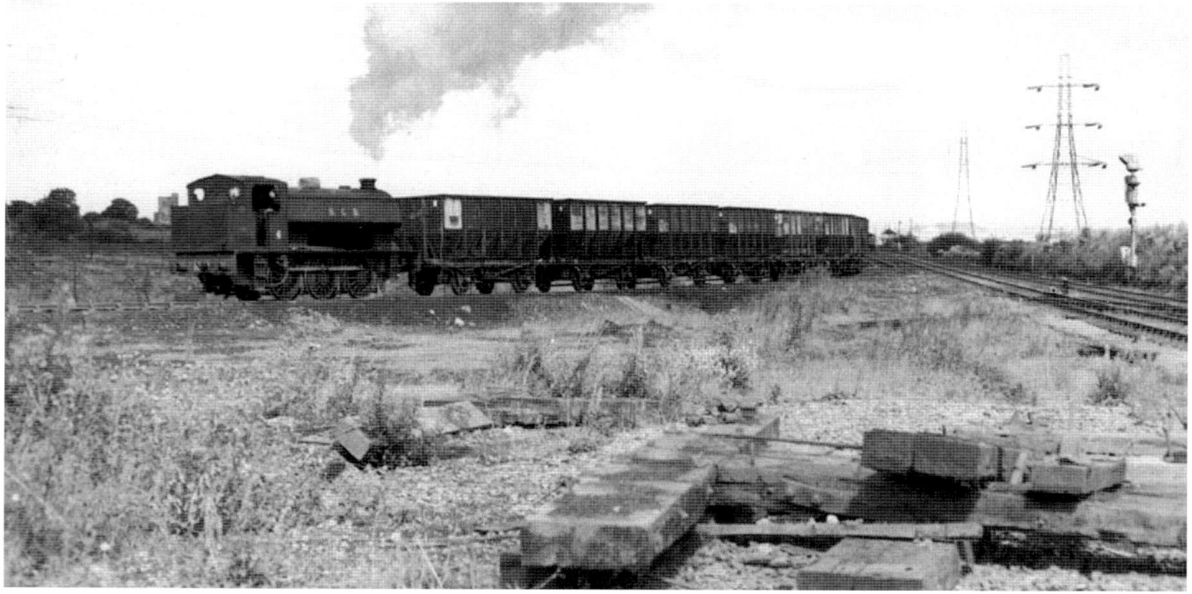

A couple of minutes later, No. 6 swings away from the BR line towards Eccles Colliery. Visible in the distance, to the right of the wagons, is Holywell signal box, which controlled the junction granting access to the branch leading to Burradon Colliery.

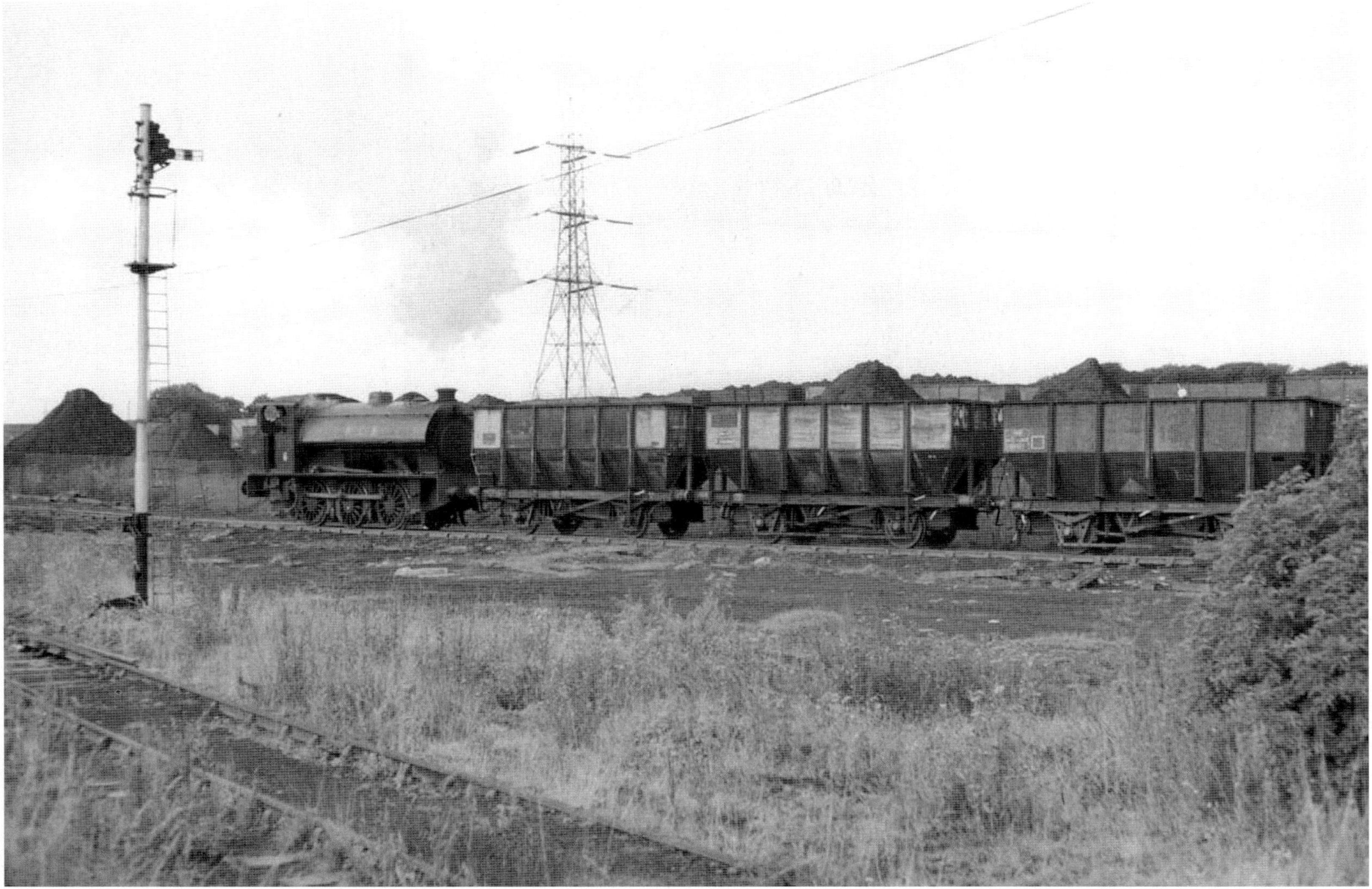

No. 6 and its train, seen again on 27 August 1974, this time passing the coal stocking site. In the foreground is the line serving Fenwick Colliery. Earsdon signal box, which housed the levers for the semaphore signal and the catch points on the left protecting the approach to the flat crossing over the Blyth & Tyne line, was just behind the photographer.

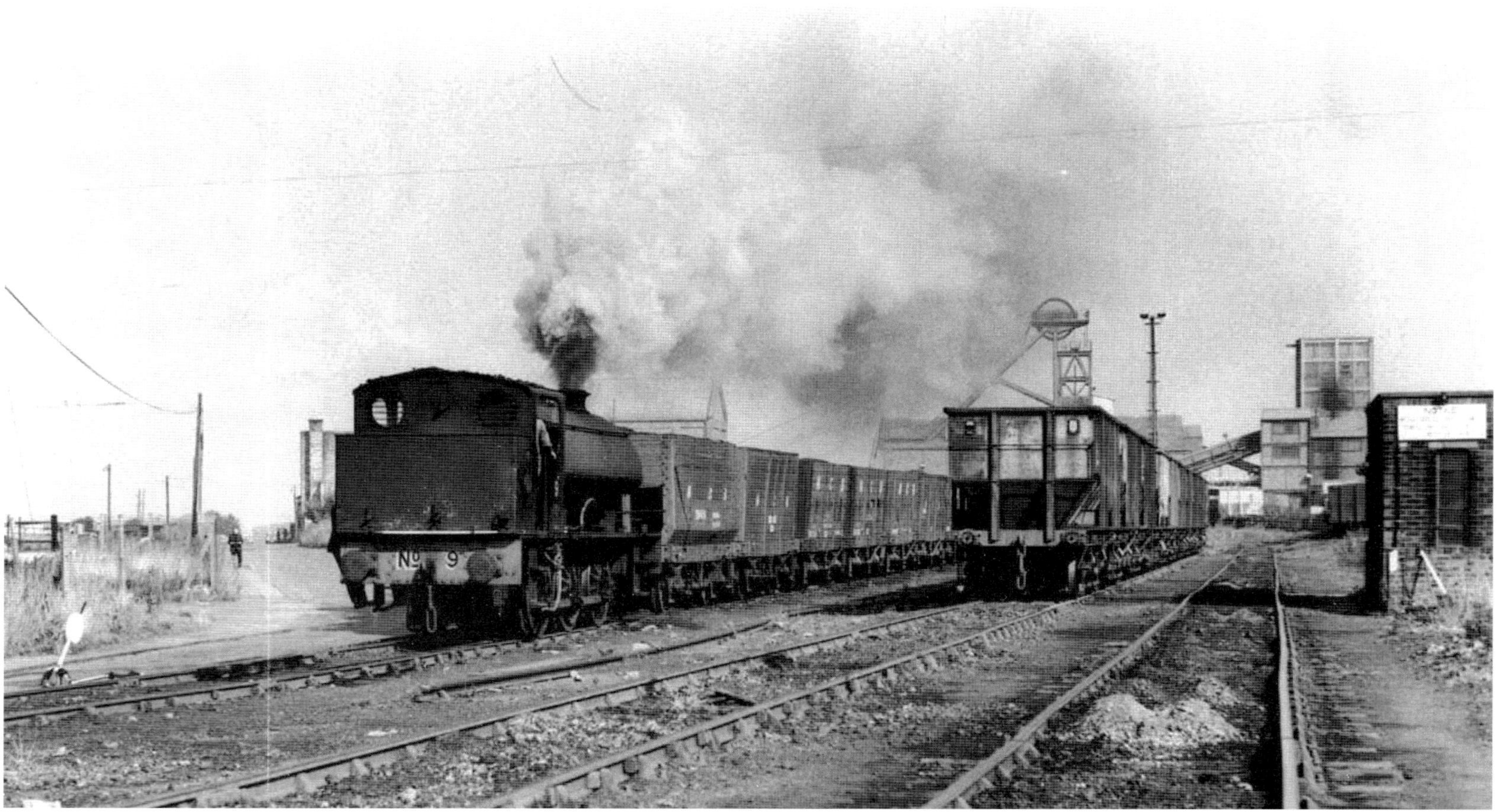

Fenwick Colliery was sunk on the site of an earlier mine in 1860. In 1947 some 225,000 tons of coal was brought to the surface and sold for gas, household, manufacturing and steam purposes, the office staff preparing the wage packets for 810 men. The official returns for 1962 record a slightly increased output of 245,000 tons, with 655 men listed on the payroll. Unbeknown at the time this and the following photographs were taken at Fenwick on 1 September 1972, the mine had just entered its final year of production; the very last shift of all was to return to the surface on 31 August 1973. Here, Robert Stephenson & Hawthorns 'Austerity' 0-6-0ST works No. 7097, NCB No. 9, drags some wooden-bodied wagons away from the pit head. The engine had started life locally in the maker's Forth Banks Works in Newcastle-upon-Tyne in August 1943, from where it was despatched to the Melbourne Military Railway, a few miles south of Derby, as WD No. 75061. It arrived back in Northumberland at the Blue Bell opencast disposal point, just south of Backworth, in September 1946, and apart from a period of about three years from 1958 at the Newbattle opencast site, near Dalkeith, Midlothian, it remained in the county of its birth until the end of its colliery days. It was allocated to Backworth loco shed from December 1971.

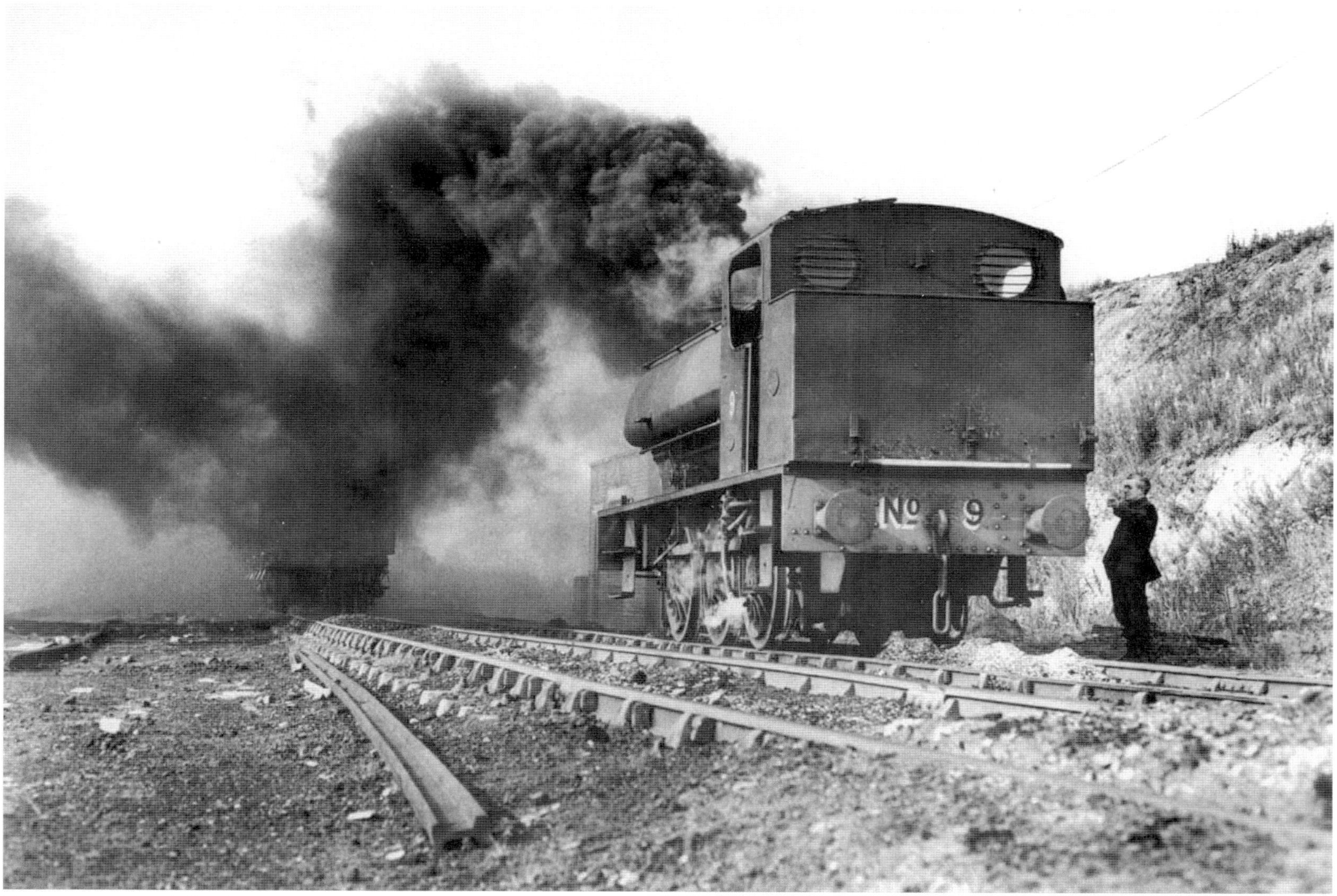

Blackout at Fenwick. While the driver makes time for conversation, No. 9 pays scant regard to the provisions of the 1956 Clean Air Act as it waits by the weighbridge before returning to Eccles Colliery. Since 1976 the engine has been on the stocklist of the Strathspey Railway at Aviemore in the Scottish Highlands.

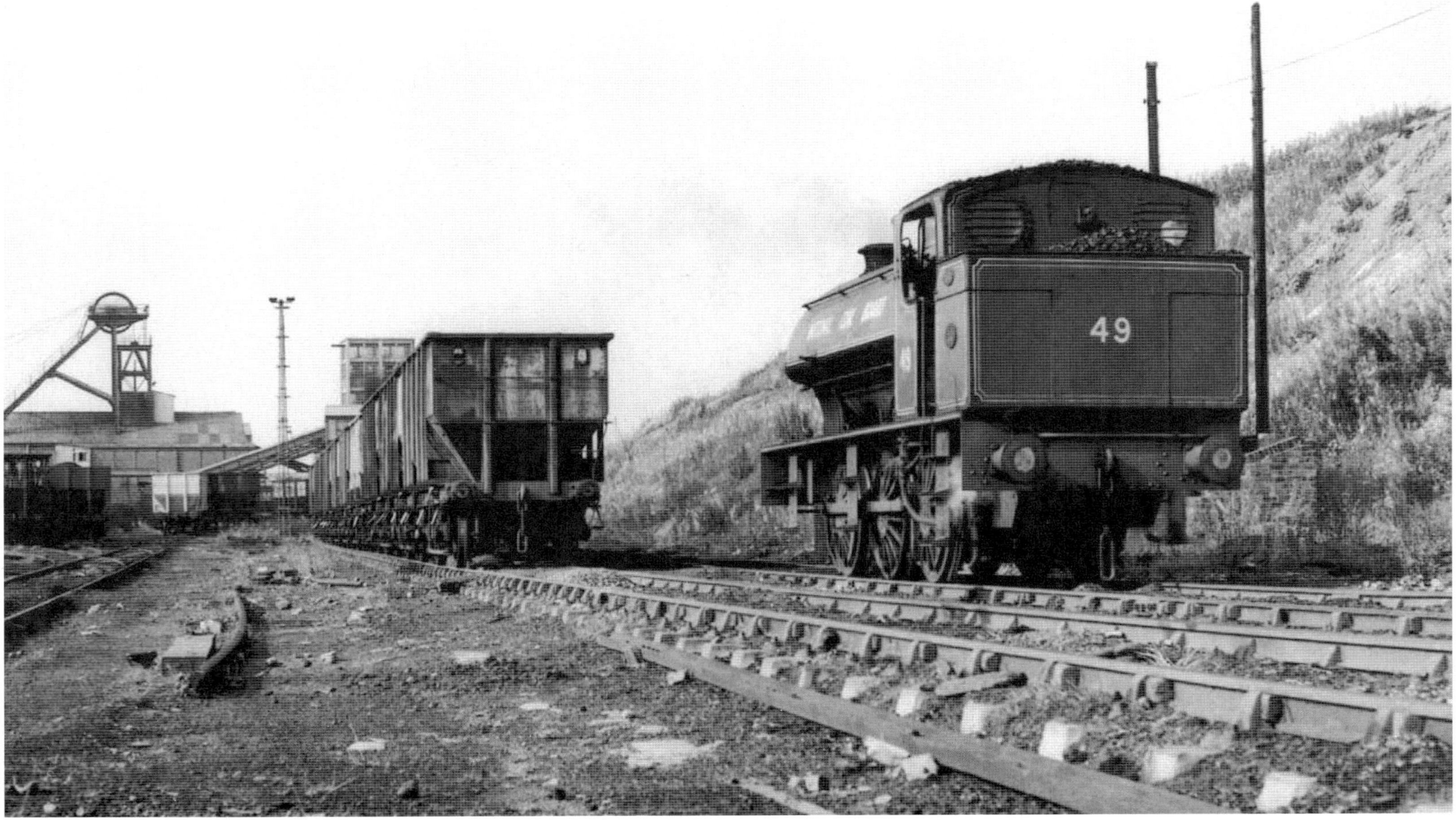

With evidence as to its ownership boldly inscribed on the saddle tank and neatly lined-out, 'Austerity' NCB No. 49 bides time at Fenwick Colliery on 1 September 1972. The engine had in fact followed NCB No. 9, seen on the previous two pages, off the Robert Stephenson & Hawthorns assembly lines in August 1943 as works No. 7098, WD No. 75062, and like its slightly older sister was forwarded to the Melbourne Military Railway. Later, after an Army posting to Shoeburyness in Essex, and to a couple of opencast sites in the Midlands under the direction of the Ministry of Fuel & Power, it rejoined its former companion at the Blue Bell opencast site in April 1947, transferring its affections to the nearby NCB Backworth shed in December 1959.

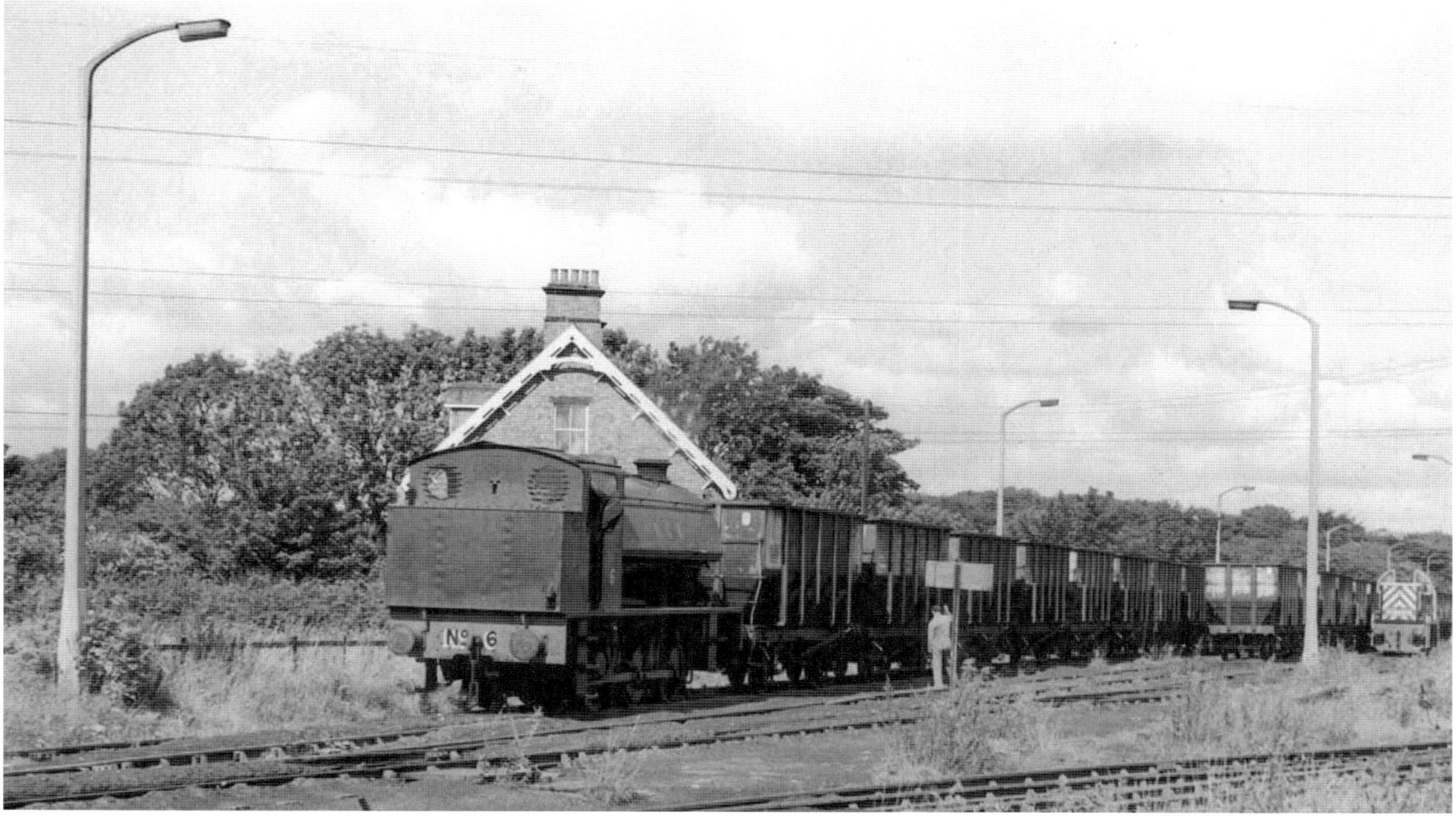

Returning to the south end of Eccles Colliery on 27 August 1974, the shunter watches closely as the driver of No. 6 carefully pushes some empty wagons towards the pit head. The tracks in the right foreground led to the BR exchange sidings and Fenwick Colliery, although these became obsolete in 1975 when, much to the relief of many motorists, a new east to north spur was installed, bringing to an end the need for frequent shunting movements back and forth over the nearby level crossing (see page 13). Interloper on the right is a former British Railways Class 14 diesel-hydraulic 0-6-0 on a visit from the Burradon Colliery system. In total fifty-six of these locomotives were built for the Western Region at Swindon Works during 1964/65, but by April 1969 they had all been withdrawn. Forty-eight were subsequently purchased by industrial concerns, nineteen eventually finding homes at NCB locations in the North East, with nine being employed at various times on the Backworth/Burradon network of lines. In August 1974 Nos. D9502, D9513, D9535, D9540 and D9555 were based at the latter. The Class 14s took command at Backworth when steam finished at the end of 1975.

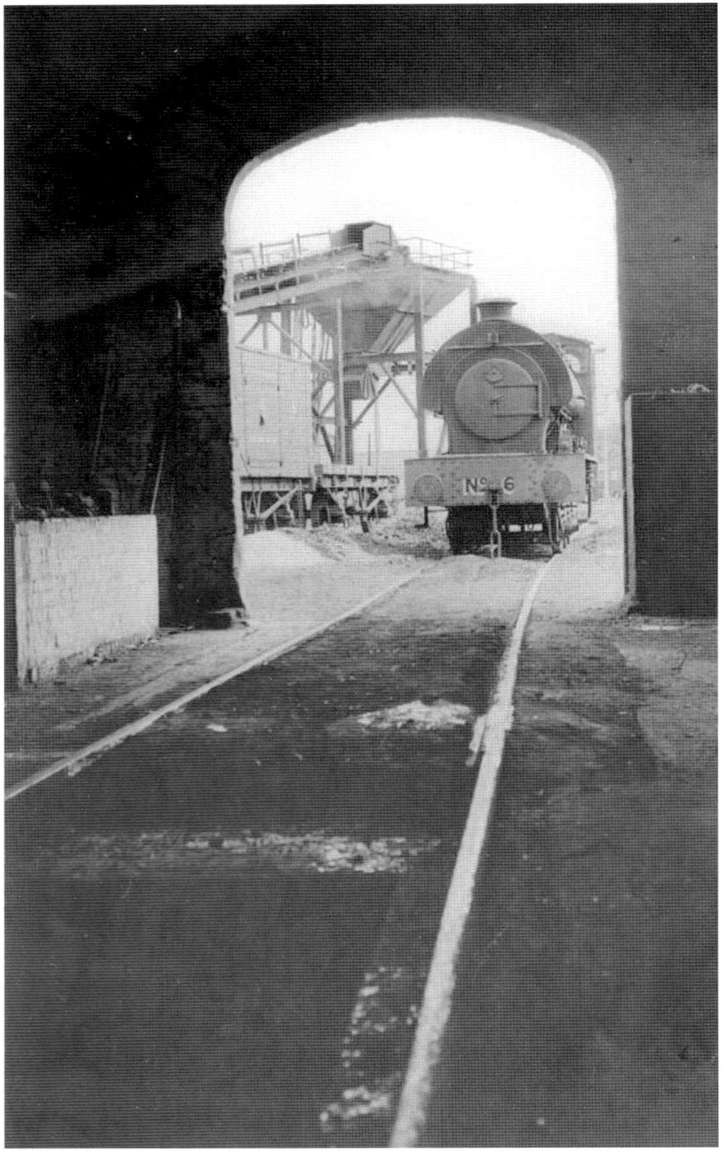

Before retiring for the night, No. 6 pauses outside the arched-entrance to the brick-built engine shed at Eccles Colliery on 27 August 1974. The tool van and the bolster wagon stabled on the adjacent siding were available for the track maintenance gang. The conveyor-fed hopper in the background, erected by the NCB, was used to replenish the locomotives' bunkers. Previously, as at the vast majority of collieries, the engines had to be coaled by hand.

Opposite: Inside the well-appointed two-road shed on the same day, No. 6 stands over the pits alongside three fellow 0-6-0STs. No. 6 first left Bagnall's Castle Engine Works in Stafford (works No. 2749) thirty years earlier in August 1944 as WD No. 75161, destined for the Central Ordnance Depot at Donnington in Shropshire. Within three months it had been assigned to the Ministry of Fuel & Power West Hallam opencast site in Derbyshire, staying there until July 1961 when it became a resident of Backworth.

At the far end of the adjacent road, the partly obscured 'Austerity' No. 48, was a Hunslet-built example (works No. 2864). It first went to the Base Ordnance Depot at Bicester in Oxfordshire as WD No. 75015 in August 1943. From December 1945, following a fifteen-month period of enforced idleness in store on the Melbourne Military Railway, it was employed at the Moorthorpe opencast site, between Wakefield and Doncaster. After working briefly at two further coal outlets, first in Nottinghamshire and then back in Yorkshire, it was transported north during the spring of 1949 to the Blue Bell opencast disposal point at Backworth. It was transferred the short distance to the main Backworth shed in December 1959. The history of the other 'Austerity' on view, No. 49, is detailed on page 18.

Sandwiched between the two 'Austerities' on the right is NCB No. 16, a Robert Stephenson & Hawthorns-built 0-6-0ST, works No. 7944. It was originally supplied in December 1957 as an oil-fired engine to the NCB East Cramlington locomotive shed, just to the north of Backworth. It was reallocated to Bedlington 'A' Colliery, south of Ashington, in March 1962, and then to Backworth in October 1971. Fitted with 18in. x 24in. outside cylinders and 4ft 0in. diameter wheels, tractive effort when calculated at 85% of the maximum boiler pressure of 180lb. per square inch was 24,786lb. This was marginally in excess of the 'Austerities', which had a tractive effort of 23,870lb.

Remarkably, all four engines on view have survived into the twenty-first century, Nos. 16 and 49 not too far away from their old haunts on the Tanfield Railway at Marley Hill, south-west of Gateshead, on the other side of the River Tyne in County Durham, while both Nos. 6 and 48 are comfortably settled north of the border in Scotland, the former on the Caledonian Railway at Brechin in Angus, the latter on the Strathspey Railway at Aviemore, where it continues to keep company with No. 9 (see page 17).

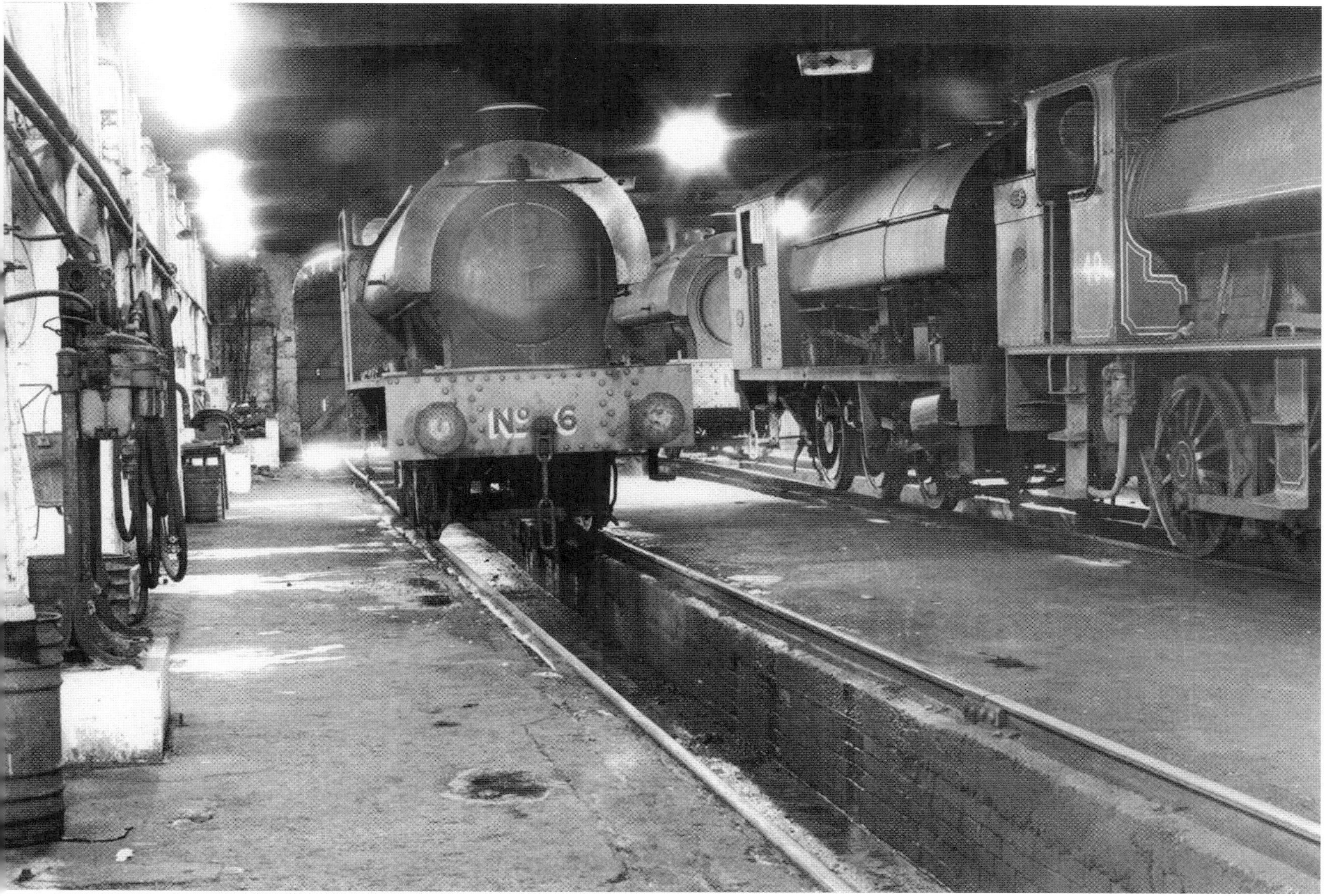
No 6

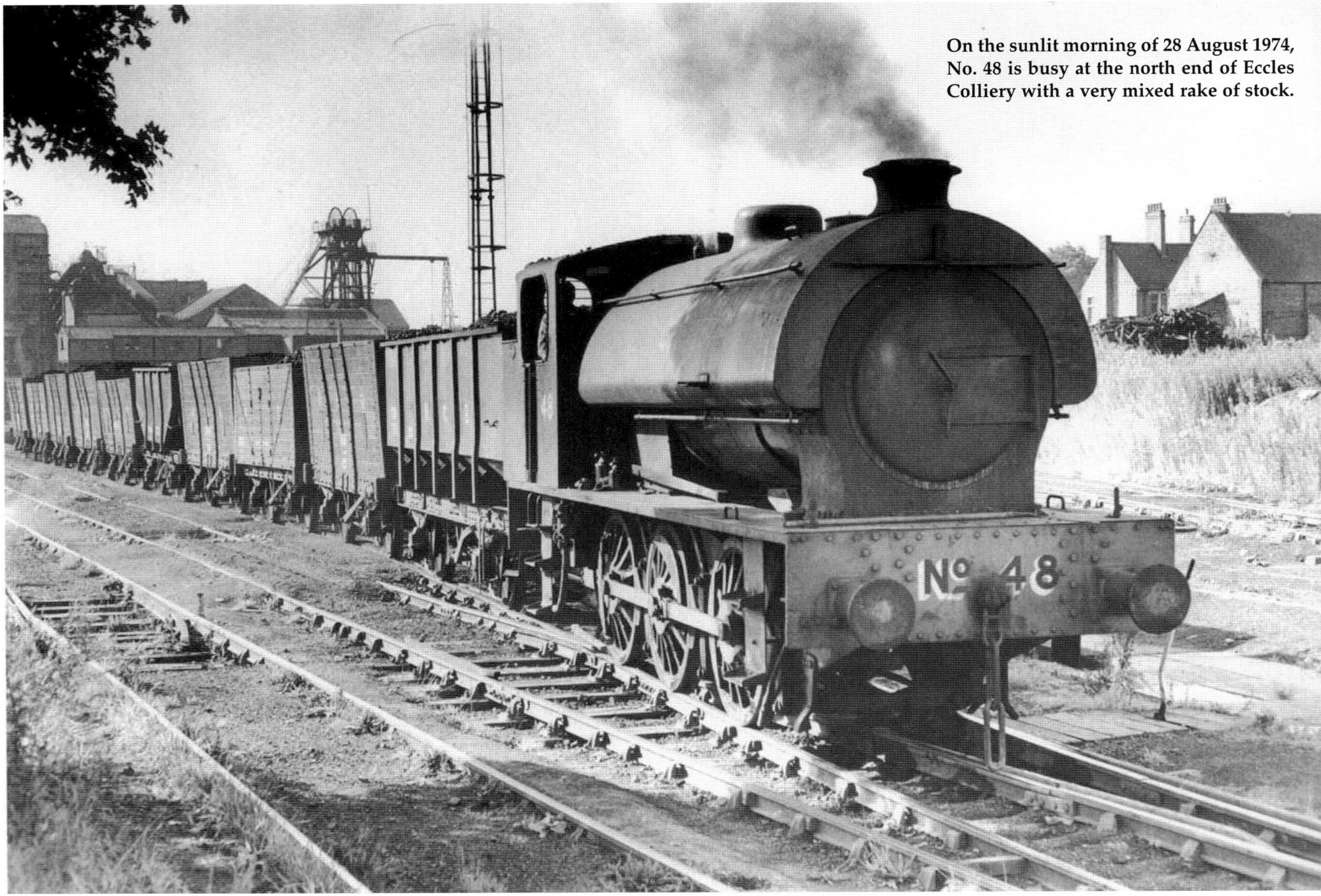

On the sunlit morning of 28 August 1974, No. 48 is busy at the north end of Eccles Colliery with a very mixed rake of stock.

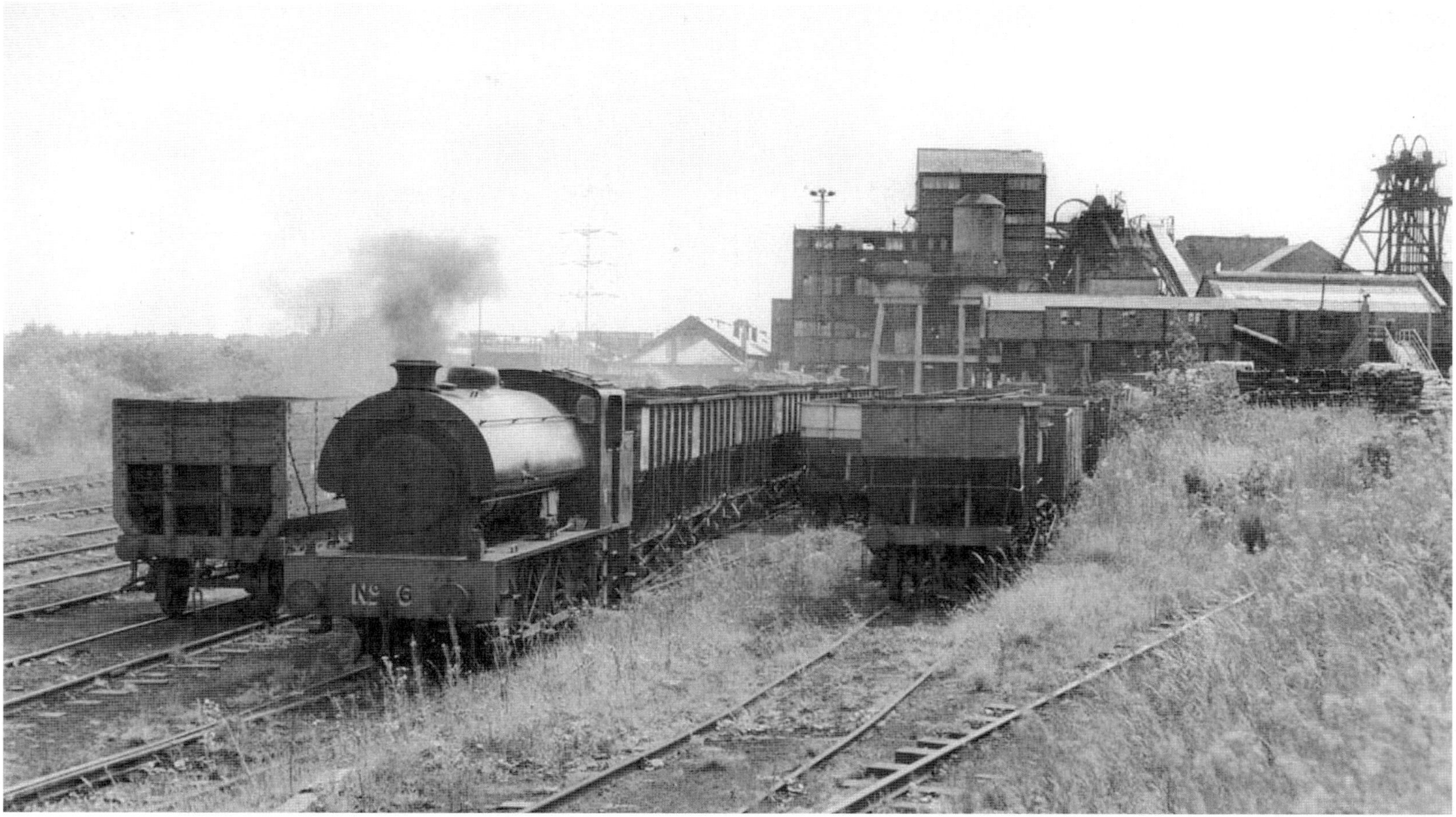

The previous day No. 6 was captured on film amidst the somewhat weed-infested yard at Eccles Colliery. The coal preparation plant, built during the 1930s, incorporated a barium washer and dryer, the mineral providing another source of income. Although the plant partially collapsed in 1970, rendering it useless, one of the two barium hoppers was still in evidence beyond the wagons on the right. The roof of the engine shed can be seen above the leading three wagons behind No. 6. The cages attached to the winding wheels on the right plunged to a maximum depth of 1,440 feet and were first used to raise coal in 1907. Forty years later, during 1947, they lifted over 210,000 tons at a time when 550 men laboured underground with the backup of a further 180 on the surface. Eccles was the last of the former influential Backworth Coal Company pits to remain in production, the final tubs from below ground being emptied in May 1980. The area in the immediate foreground was later redeveloped for housing, while the rest of the site, apart from the workshops which have been taken over by a variety of small businesses, remains derelict.

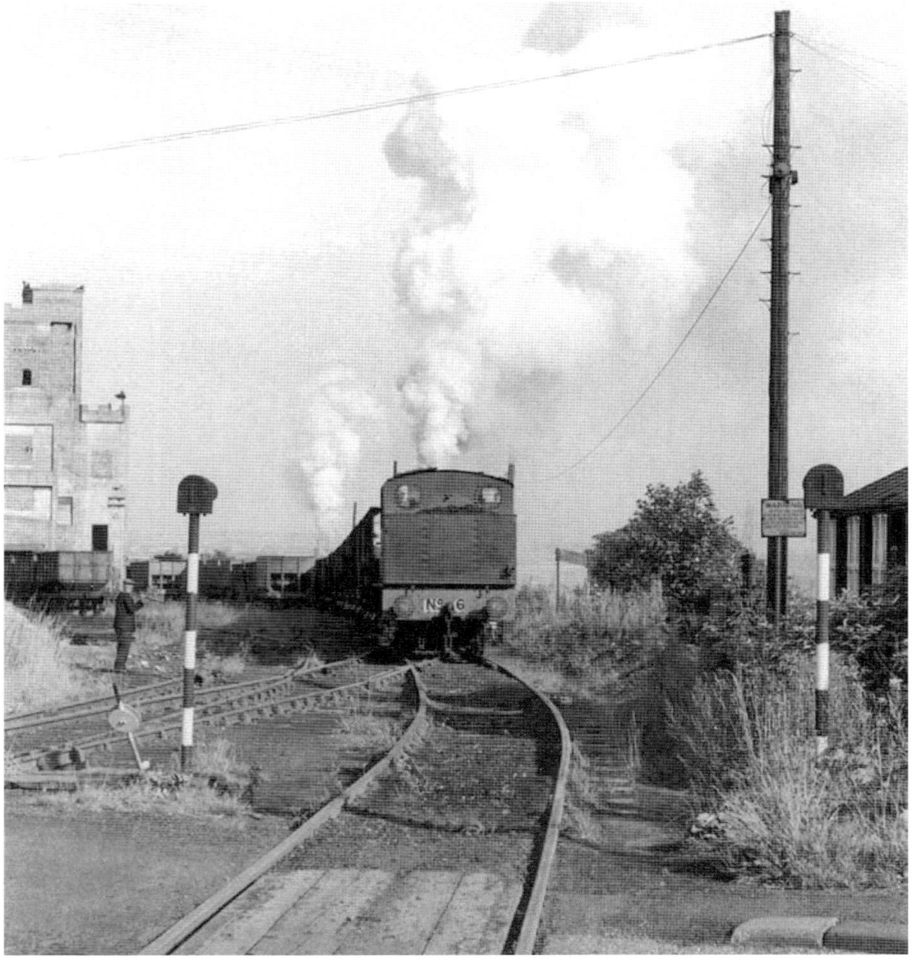

Maximum effort is exerted by both Nos. 6 and 48 as they toil fore and aft of a lengthy train nearing 'School Crossing', at the north end of Eccles Colliery, on 28 August 1974. Note the strategically placed colour-light signals at the approach to the level crossing. The castellated building on the left, on the site of the old Backworth 'B' Colliery which closed back in the 1890s, were the remains of a washery - 'the Dolly Washer'. Latterly it was used as a wagon shop.

As No. 6 storms up to the ungated crossing the keeper displays a rather tatty red flag against any oncoming vehicles.

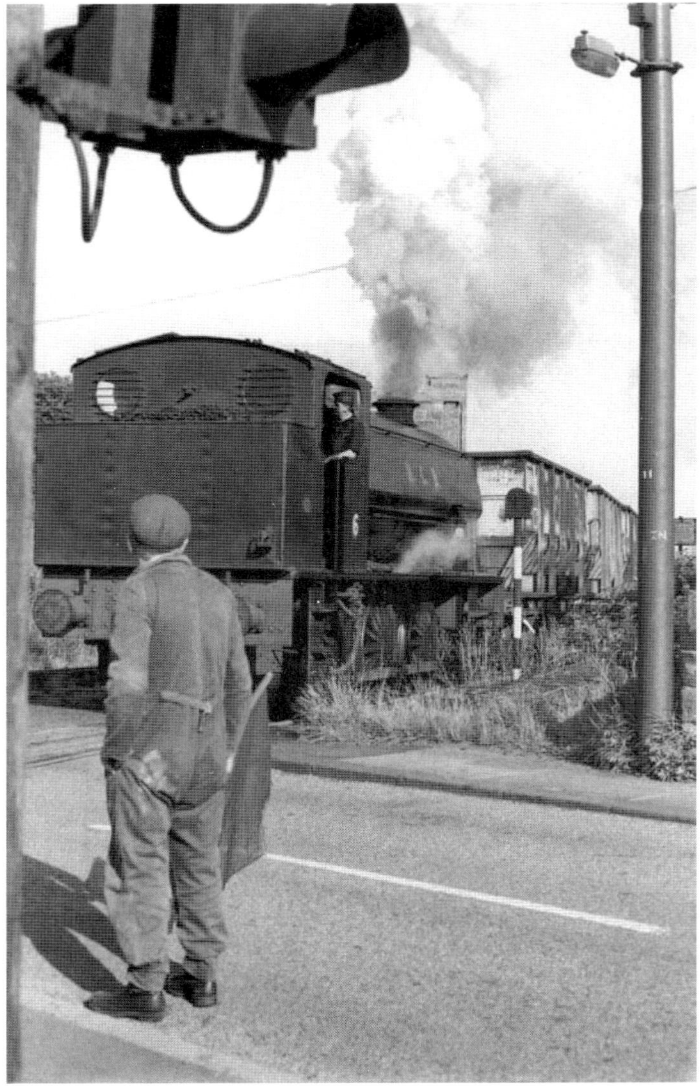

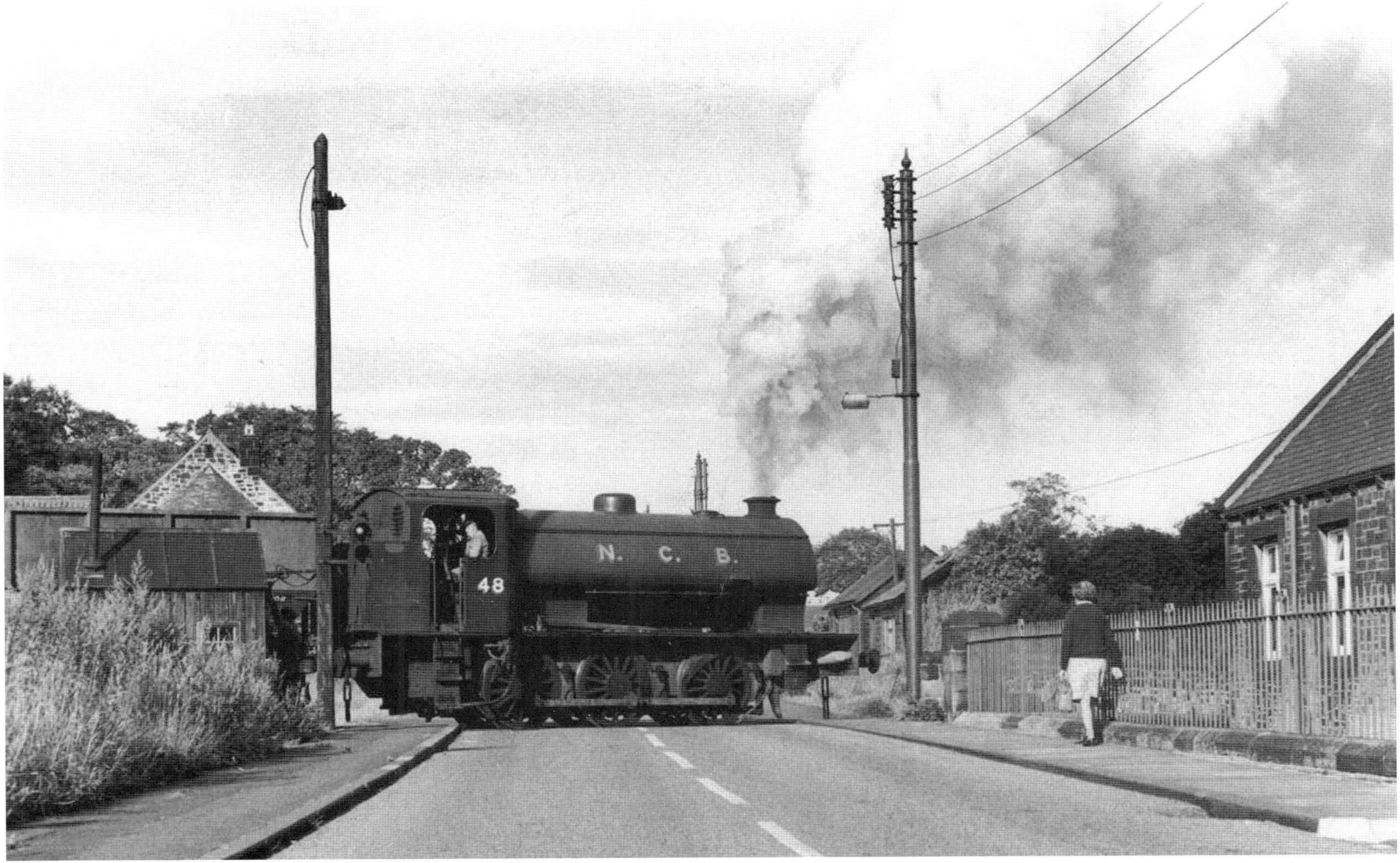

The red road traffic signal continues to shine as No. 48 blasts across the road at the rear of the convoy, while the crossing keeper retires to his wooden cabin. It would appear that the facilities provided here were not quite as salubrious as those inhabited by his mate at the south end of the colliery as depicted on page 13. The school building (since demolished) that gave its name to the crossing is visible on the right. The trackbed north of this point has been converted to a footpath and in deference to its original purpose is officially known as the Backworth Waggonway. It is clearly signposted to 'C' Pit ¾ mile and Seghill 1½ mile.

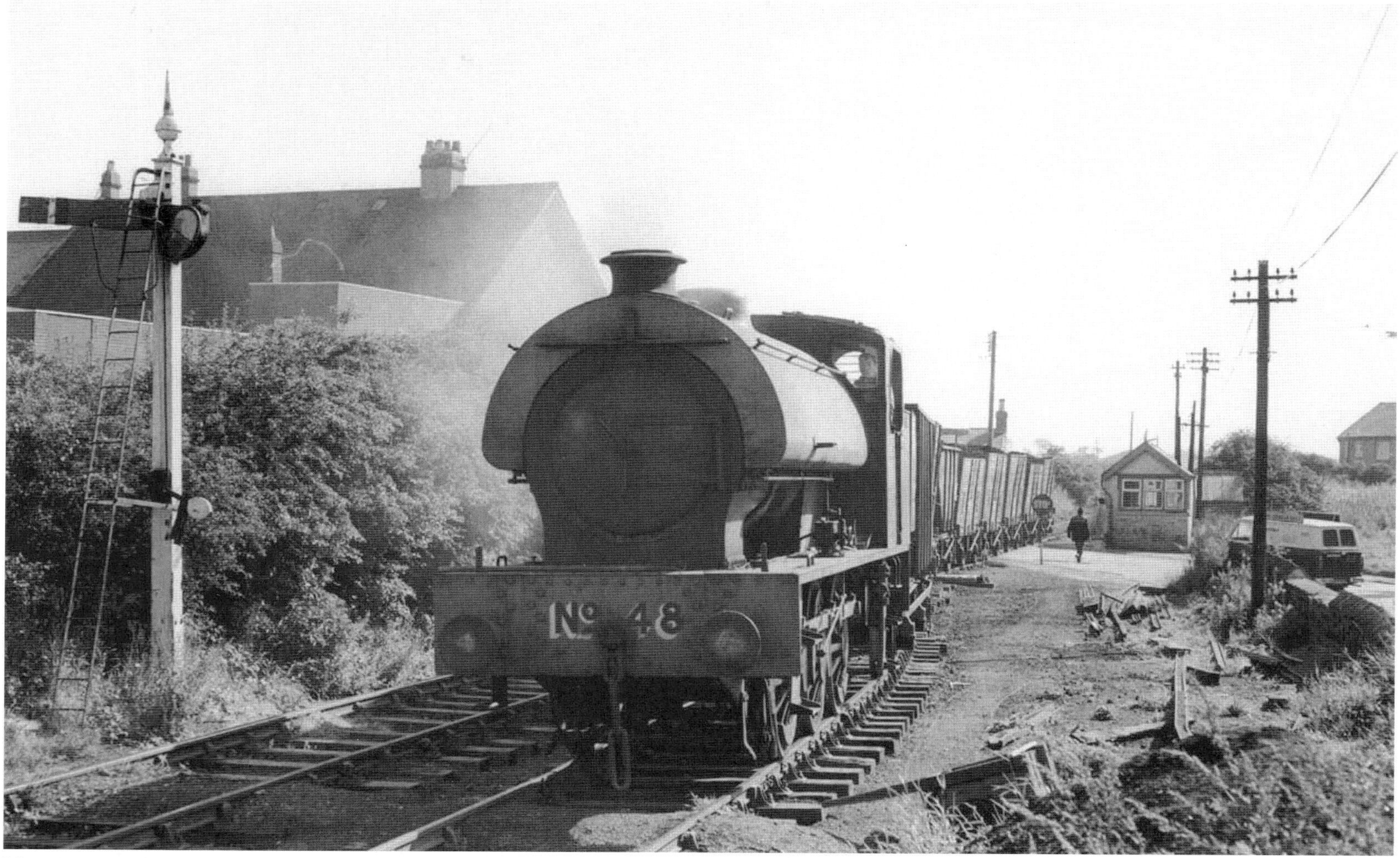

No. 48 enters the passing loop at Burradon village, two miles west of Backworth, while hauling coal from Eccles Colliery to Weetslade Central Coal Preparation Plant for washing on 28 August 1974. The crossing keeper is already on his way back to his cabin, having turned the hand-operated 'stop' sign through ninety degrees so as to face the railway rather than the road. Through running between the Backworth and Burradon colliery networks only became possible in 1951, when a short connecting line to the ex-Hazlerigg & Burradon Coal Company branch from Holywell (built in 1912) was installed near Fisher Lane by the NCB (see map on page 12). Notice the wooden semaphore signal, complete with ornate finial, on the left.

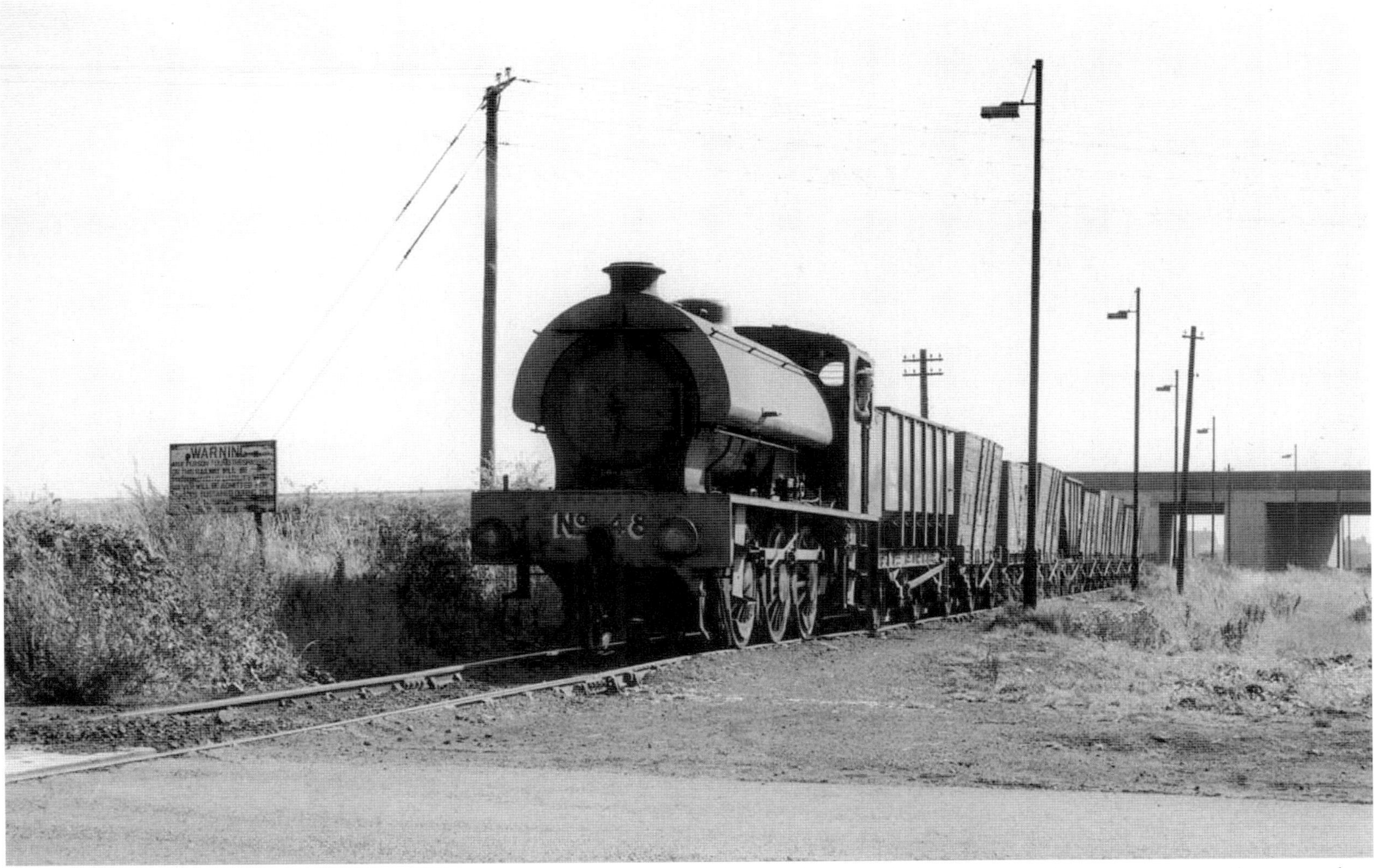

A little further into its journey on the same day and No. 48 has just emerged from under the A189 Newcastle to Bedlington road, on the approach to Weetslade. The shunter seems to be enjoying the trip as he surveys the scene from his lofty position. From 1969 any interchange traffic between Weetslade and Backworth, either coal for washing or waste material for the tip, was usually handled by one of the ex-BR Class 14 diesels (see page 19), but in 1974 a twice-weekly steam run was reintroduced. In fact towards the end of the year and early in 1975 these workings became almost a daily occurrence.

No. 48 awaits permission to cross over the B1319 road and enter the Weetslade complex. The central coal preparation facility here, to be seen in the background, along with a coal concentration depot was developed during the 1960s, the latter replacing a number of smaller landsale outlets on Tyneside. Weetslade Colliery itself closed in September 1966.

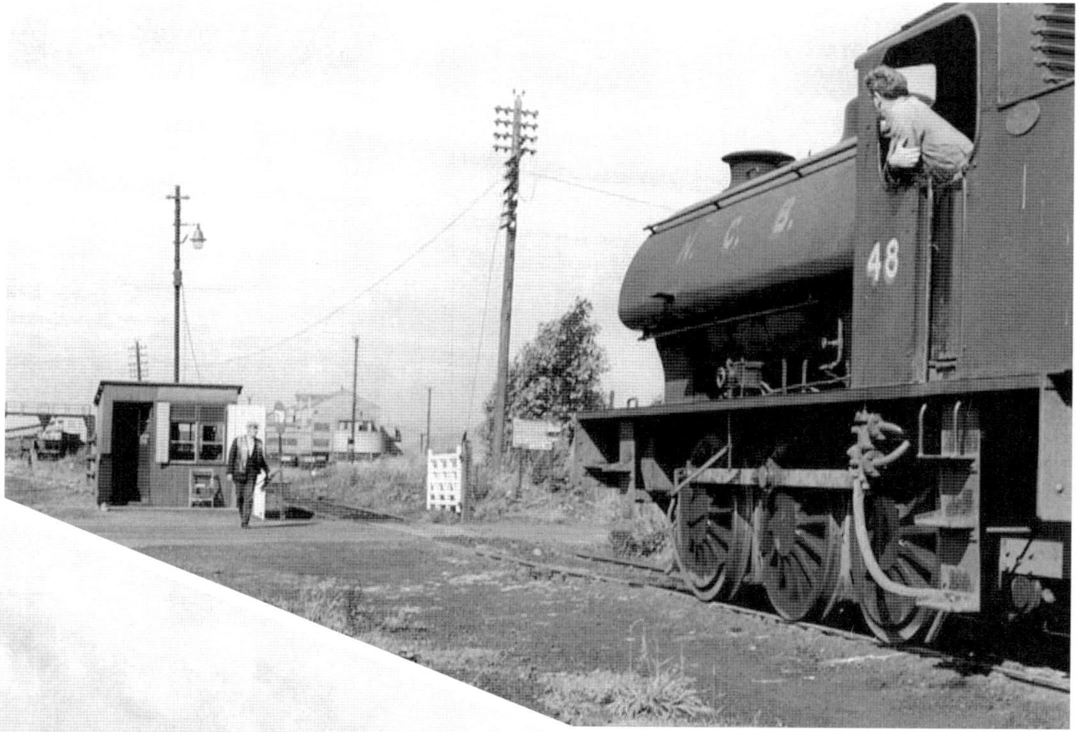

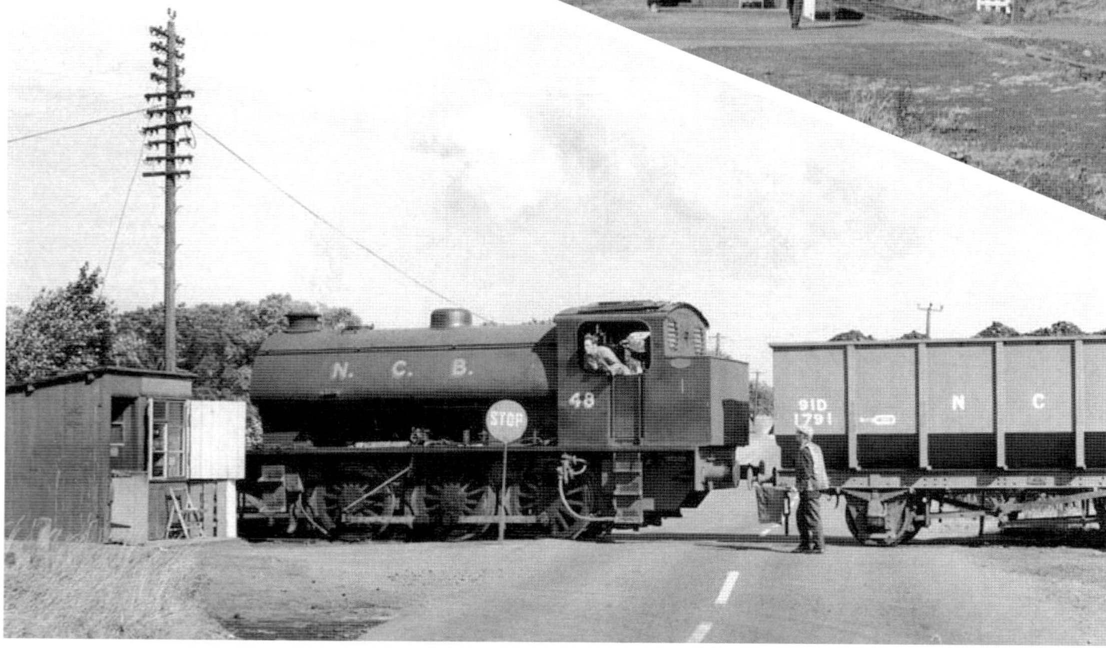

With the flag-wielding crossing keeper in the middle of the roadway and the 'stop' board correctly positioned, No. 48 next eases its rake of NCB wagons slowly towards their destination. Obviously, on a pleasantly warm day such as this, the man in charge much preferred to while away the time between trains sitting outside the cabin.

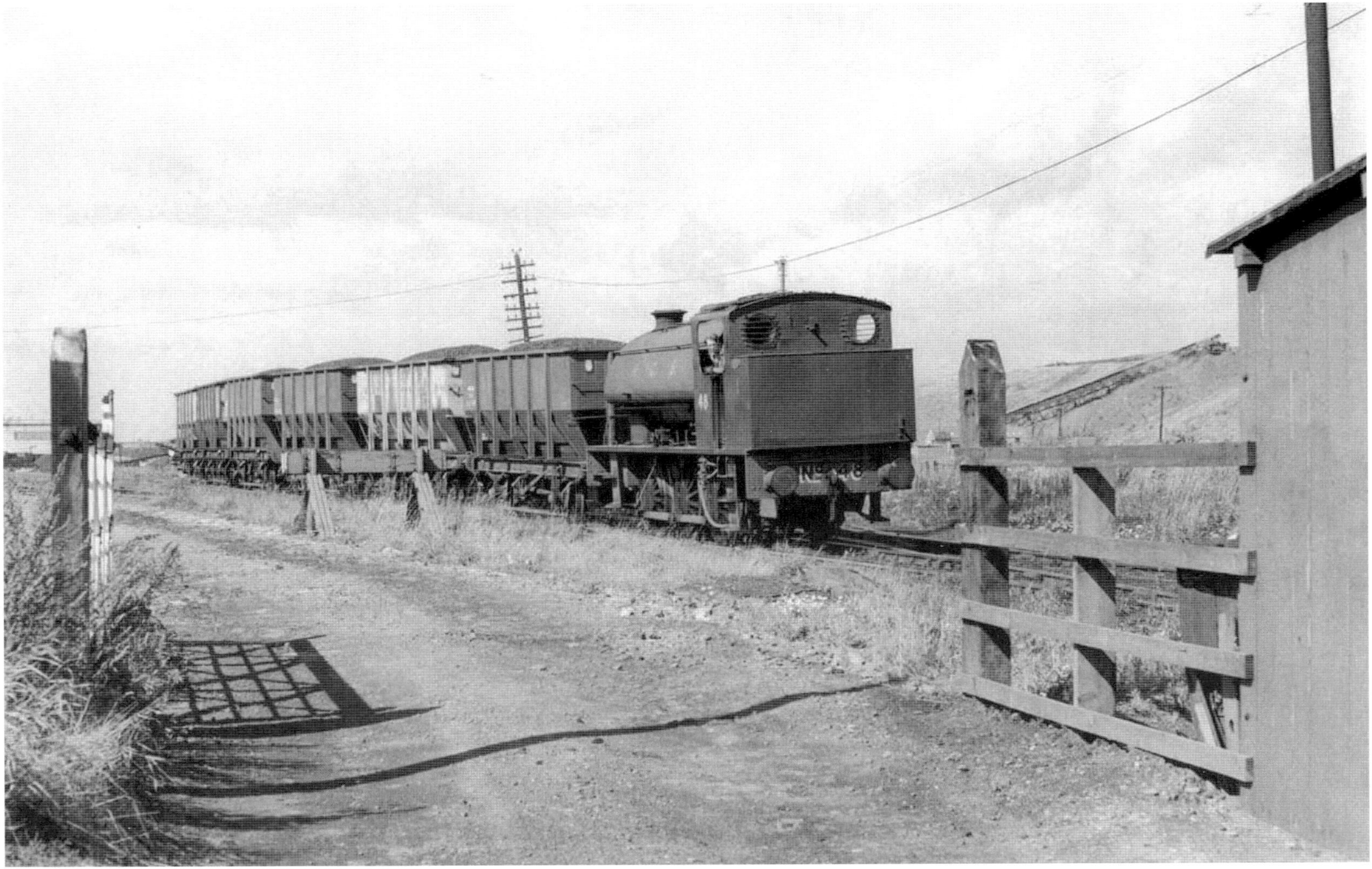

No. 48 didn't linger long at Weetslade and was soon on its way back to Eccles Colliery, this time with a set of six hopper wagons laden with washed coal. The train is about to cross the B1319 road. The plant finished in March 1981 although the link between Weetslade and Backworth was taken out of commission earlier, in November 1977. The latter now forms part of the Seaton Burn Waggonway, a designated three-and-a-quarter-mile walking and cycling route between Seaton Burn and Killingworth.

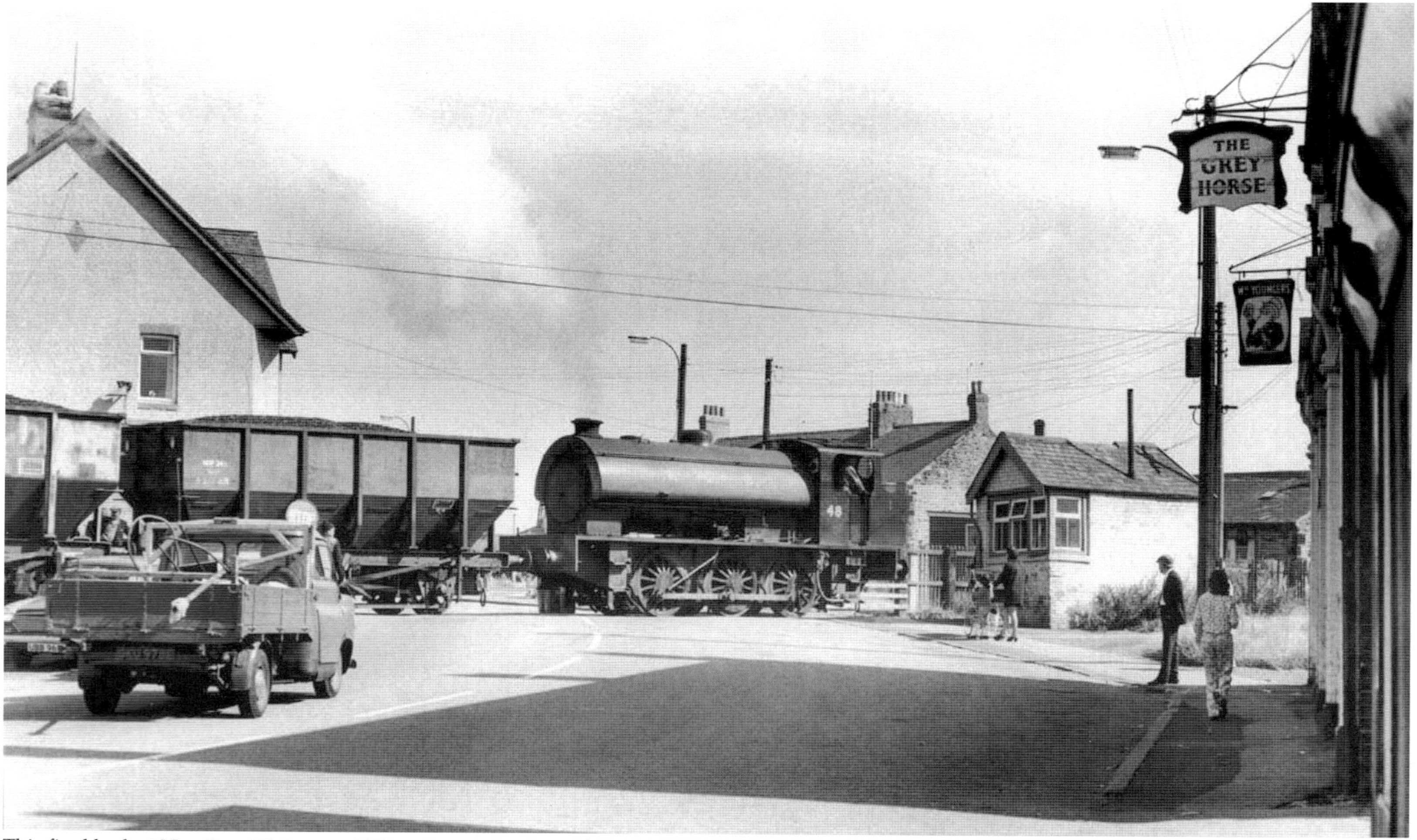

This final look at No. 48 on 28 August 1974, as it scurries through Burradon while en route to Eccles Colliery, also proved to be the last occasion the author had the pleasure of sighting a working NCB-owned steam locomotive in Northumberland. Similarly, a few pedestrians and the driver of a Bedford pick-up look on at what was once an everyday occurrence. It almost goes without saying that down the years many a miner, at the end of a hard shift underground, must have eagerly entered the portals of The Grey Horse pub on the right and consumed a pint or two of Wm Younger's ale. Today the pub still serves beer, while on the opposite side of the road, by an access point to the Seaton Burn Waggonway, an information board provides a potted history of the dismantled railway. An old mining tub is also positioned nearby.

Norwood Coking Plant was on the south side of the River Tyne at Dunston, in the western suburbs of Gateshead, in County Durham. The plant was founded by the Team By-Product Coke Co. Ltd in 1915 in order to process the coal from a number of collieries in the area. In 1930, after the original owners had gone into liquidation, the assets were taken over by Priestman Collieries Ltd. In those days the plant was able to process up to 300,000 tons of coal per annum in 120 Otto regenerative ovens and ten Otto combination ovens, these being replaced by the NCB in 1947 with sixty-six Simon-Carves underjet regenerative ovens. The latter had a capacity to handle up to 340,000 tons per annum. Along with the coke, the by-products of tar, sulphate of ammonia, crude benzole and gas for town use were also produced.

Nestling inside the two-road, brick-built engine shed on 28 August 1974 is Robert Stephenson & Hawthorns 0-6-0ST works No. 7412, NCB No. 77 'Norwood', which graced the plant from new in August 1948. It had 3ft 8in. diameter wheels and 16in. x 24in. outside cylinders. From the late-1960s the extensive sidings were usually shunted by diesel locomotives, although 'Norwood' continued to be maintained in good condition and was regularly steamed as the spare engine until the ovens were finally extinguished in 1980. Ten years later, in 1990, the site was utilised for the National Garden Festival before it was redeveloped for residential purposes. 'Norwood' still resides in County Durham, now in the care of the Weardale Railway at Wolsingham, some ten miles to the north-west of Bishop Auckland.

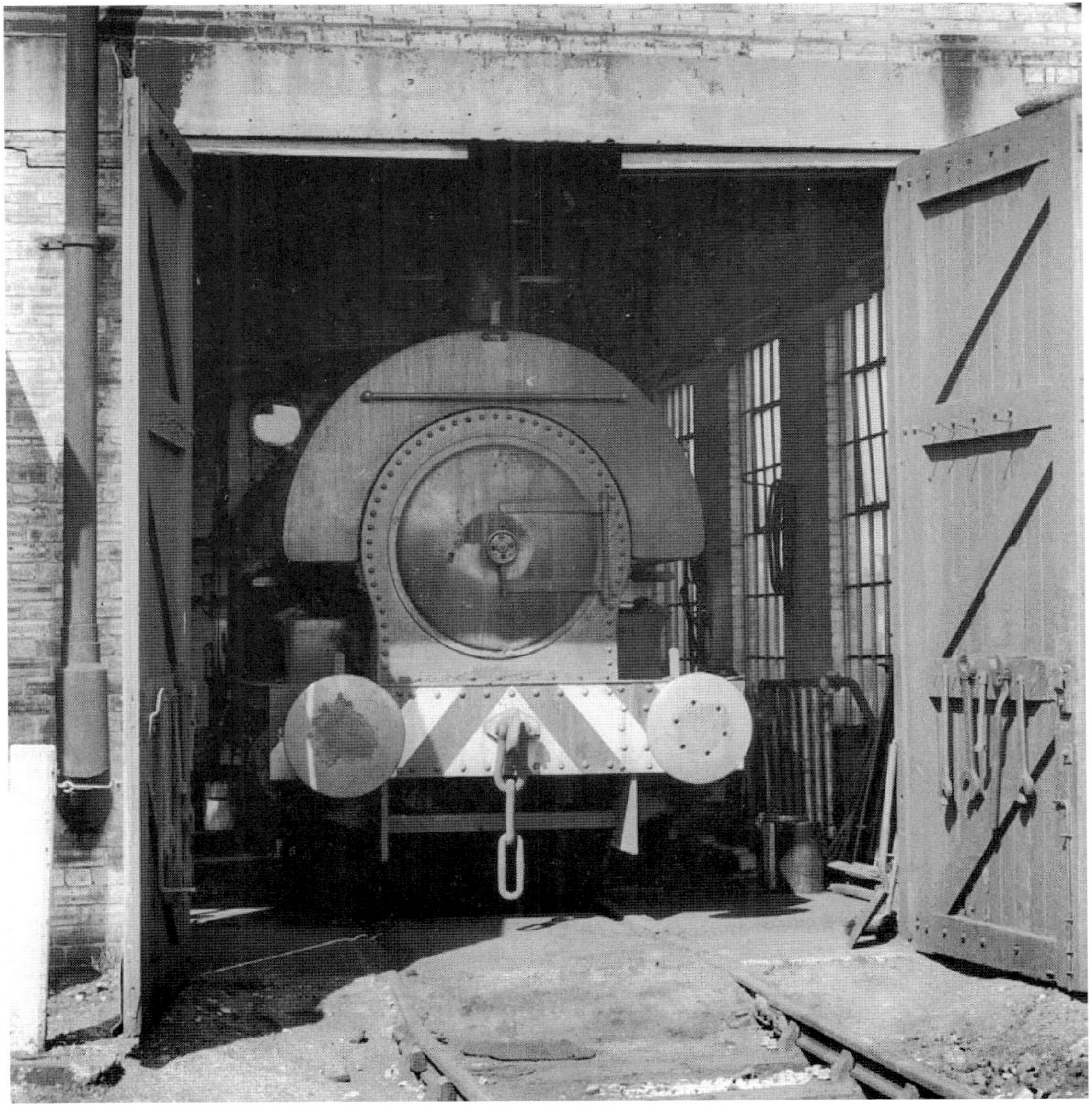

On 30 August 1972, Andrew Barclay 0-4-0ST works No. 1659, NCB No. 32, built in 1920 with 3ft 5in. diameter wheels and 14in. x 22in. outside cylinders, pushes eight wagons across the long concrete viaduct that straddled the Team Valley Trading Estate, just south of Gateshead, with coal brought to the surface at the site of Ravensworth Park Drift Mine. The viaduct was erected when the trading estate was established during the late 1930s, the first such in the United Kingdom. Beneath the viaduct a range of 1960s-registered Austin, Morris, Ford and Vauxhall cars, amongst others, belonging to workers at an adjacent factory, are parked up for the day. The line once formed part of the Pelaw Main Railway, which linked a number of inland pits to the Pelaw Main staithes on the River Tyne near Hebburn, between Gateshead and South Shields, although by this time the remaining section had been connected to the nearby Bowes Railway at Blackham's Hill. The Ravensworth Park Drift Mine, opened in 1936, had officially closed in May 1968, but subsequently the coal mined at Ravensworth Ann Colliery was brought to the surface here. This arrangement ceased and the railway closed when Ravensworth Ann was linked underground with Kibblesworth Colliery on the Bowes Railway in April 1973. No. 32 spent all its pre-nationalisation days at East Tanfield Colliery, Tantobie, between Gateshead and Consett, and following a number of postings during its NCB days eventually arrived at Shop Pit locomotive shed at Lamesley, which served this section of the railway, in January 1971. When it was no longer needed here it was moved to the NCB Springwell Workshops from where it was acquired for preservation. The engine is now based on the Tanfield Railway at Marley Hill.

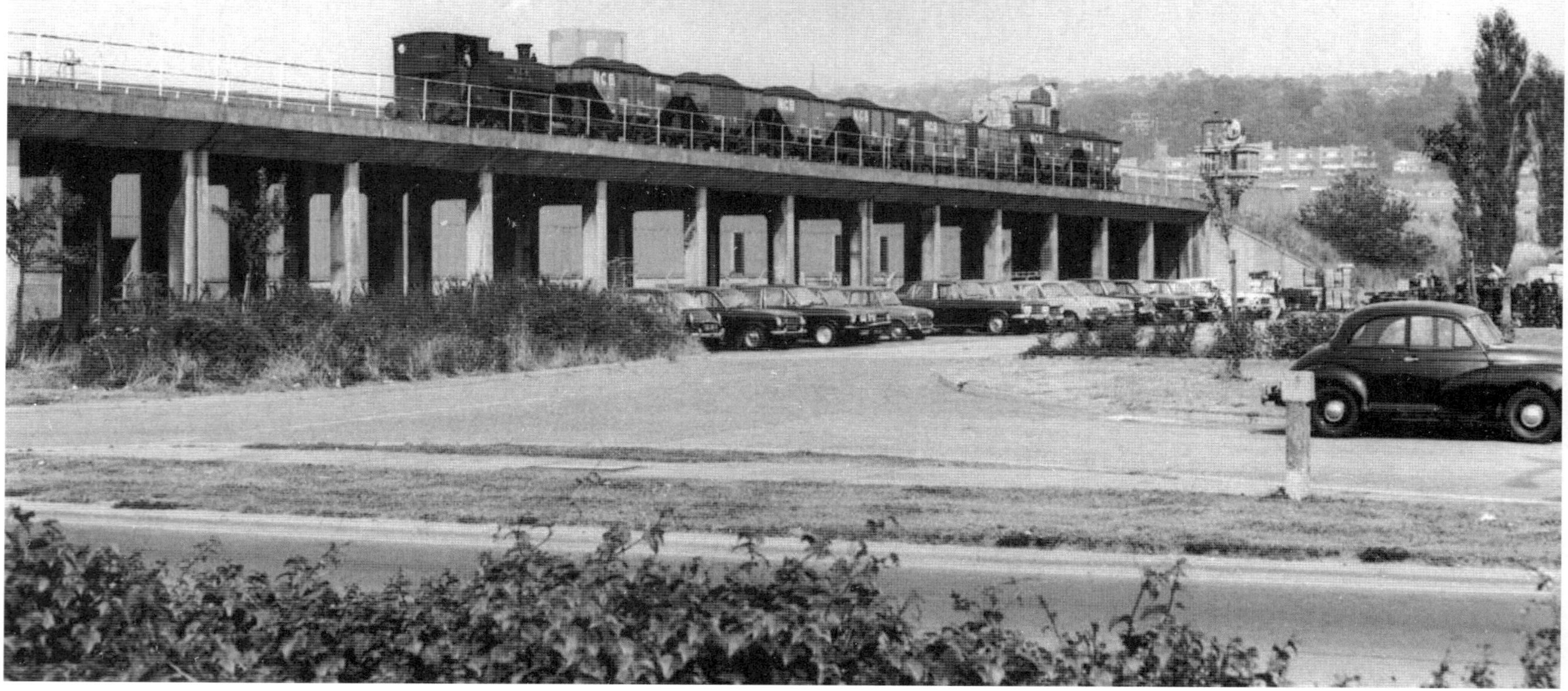

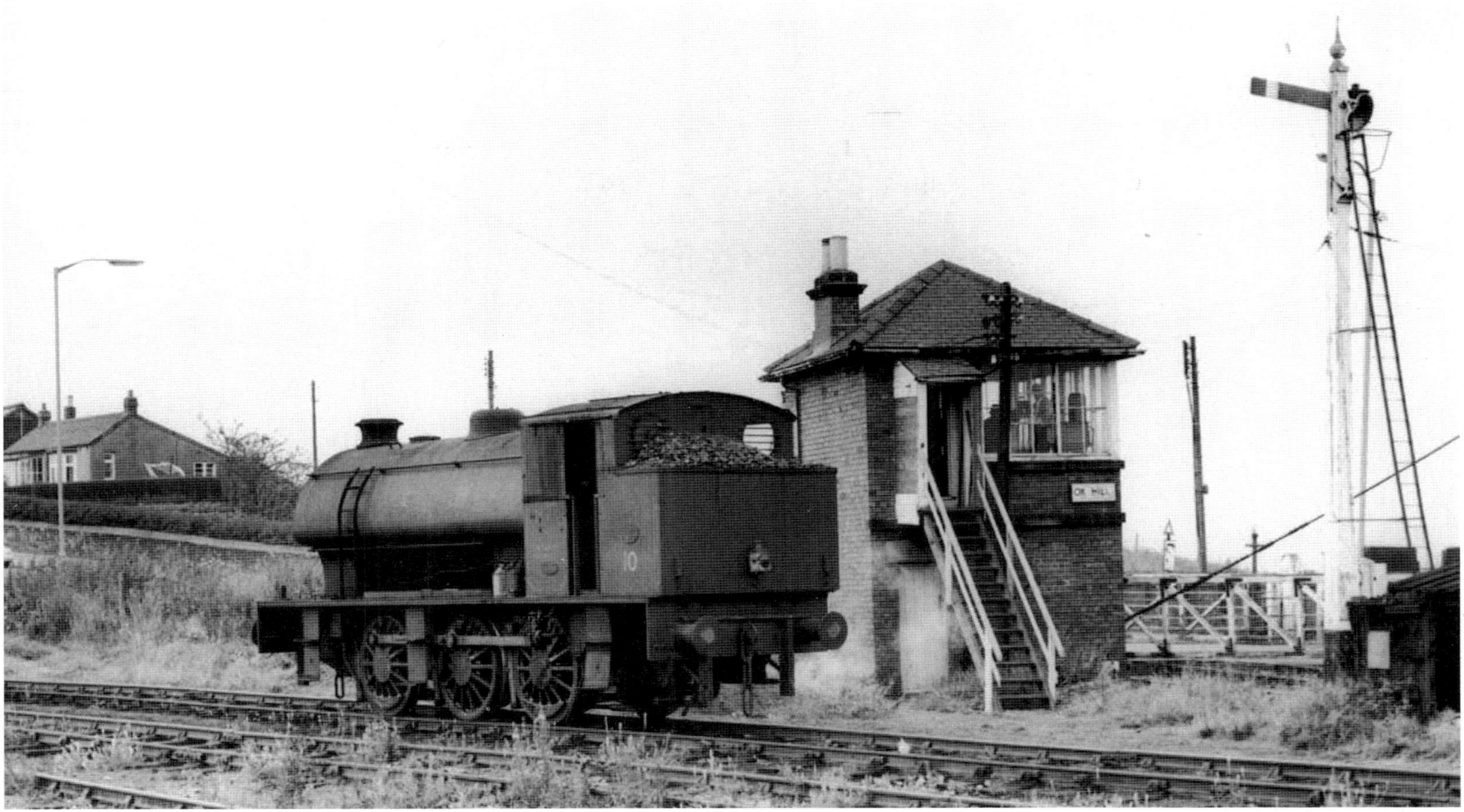

NCB No. 10, an 'Austerity' 0-6-0ST, simmers by Oxhill signal box before returning with a set of empties to Morrison Busty Colliery, Annfield Plain, on 30 August 1972. To the right of the signal box is the ex-North Eastern Railway (originally Stanhope & Tyne Railway, later Pontop & South Shields Railway) line to Consett, which lost some of its importance when a diversionary line between Pelton and Annfield Plain was opened in 1893. The old line continued to be maintained, principally to service a number of collieries, but after 1965, when Louisa Colliery, a little further to the east of Oxhill, was merged with Morrison Busty, only the section from Oxhill to Annfield East Junction remained in use. This Robert Stephenson & Hawthorns-built 'Austerity', works No. 7294, was delivered to the Longmoor Military Railway in Hampshire in September 1945 as WD No. 71485. It was sold to the NCB in April 1947, initially for use at Boldon Colliery in County Durham, before finding work at other collieries in the county prior to its transfer to Morrison Busty in February 1970. The colliery closed in October 1973 after a productive life of forty-six years, the locomotive being scrapped in July of the following year.

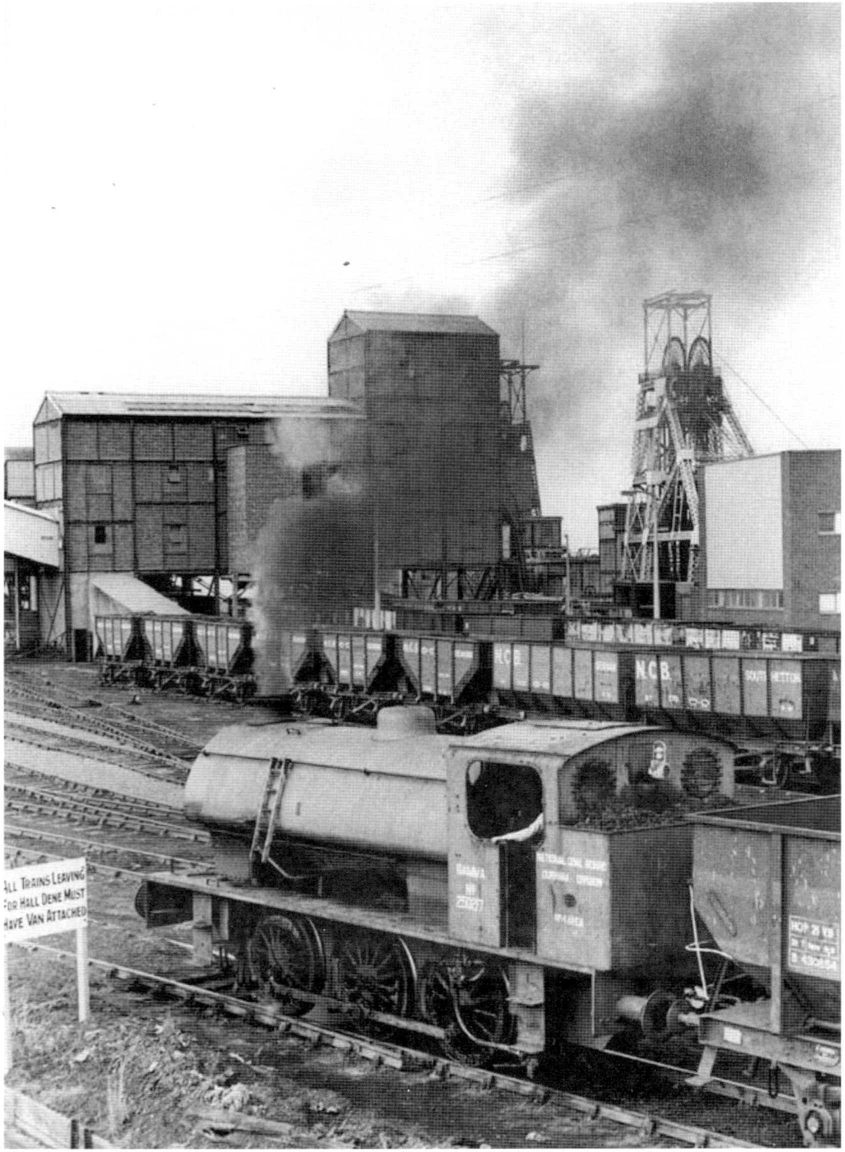

The sinking of Vane Tempest Colliery, just north of Seaham Harbour, began in February 1926, production starting in June 1929. It was owned by Londonderry Collieries Ltd, the major shareholder being the Marquess of Londonderry, whose ancestors had had considerable influence in the development of parts of the Durham coalfield over a long number of years. The colliery exploited seams that lay under the North Sea and during 1947, the industry's first year under the stewardship of the NCB, 456,000 tons of coal was hoisted up the shafts. There were then 1,820 men on the payroll, 1,429 stationed underground and 391 on the surface. By the early 1970s, following a £1 million reconstruction scheme completed in 1965, the pit was producing some 645,000 tons annually from a workforce of approximately 1,560 men.

Deputising for the usual diesel which was under repair, the working locomotive at Vane Tempest on 28 August 1974 (the day all the photographs at this colliery were taken) was NCB No. 2502/7, an 'Austerity' 0-6-0ST outshopped in June 1945 by Bagnall's of Stafford as works No. 2779, WD No. 75256. It was employed by the coal industry in Durham from April 1946, the name 'Gamma' being applied in 1964 during its time at Brandon Pit House Colliery, Brandon, near Durham itself. It was moved from there to Vane Tempest in December 1967. The details 'National Coal Board Durham Division No. 4 Area', stencilled on the side of the bunker, referred to an administrative structure that had been abolished in January 1964, indicating the engine had not seen a paint brush for over ten years. Further management reorganisations in later years culminated in the formation of the North East Area in April 1974, when all the remaining collieries in Northumberland and Durham came under one banner.

In this view, as well as a variety of wagons, above the locomotive's cab can be seen the winding wheels of the 'Vane' downcast shaft, with the 'Tempest' upcast headgear partly visible to the left. The shafts reached a depth of 1,895 feet. The instruction on the board near the front of the engine in respect of trains leaving for Hall Dene was for the benefit of BR drivers making their way back along the short branch to the junction with the Sunderland to Hartlepool main line. *Opposite*: Two workmen cycle along the path adjacent to the sidings at the south end of Vane Tempest Colliery, seemingly oblivious of 'Gamma' as it manoeuvres three steel wagons. The loaded wagons on the right are awaiting the arrival of a British Railways diesel locomotive. Beyond the residential properties lies the North Sea.

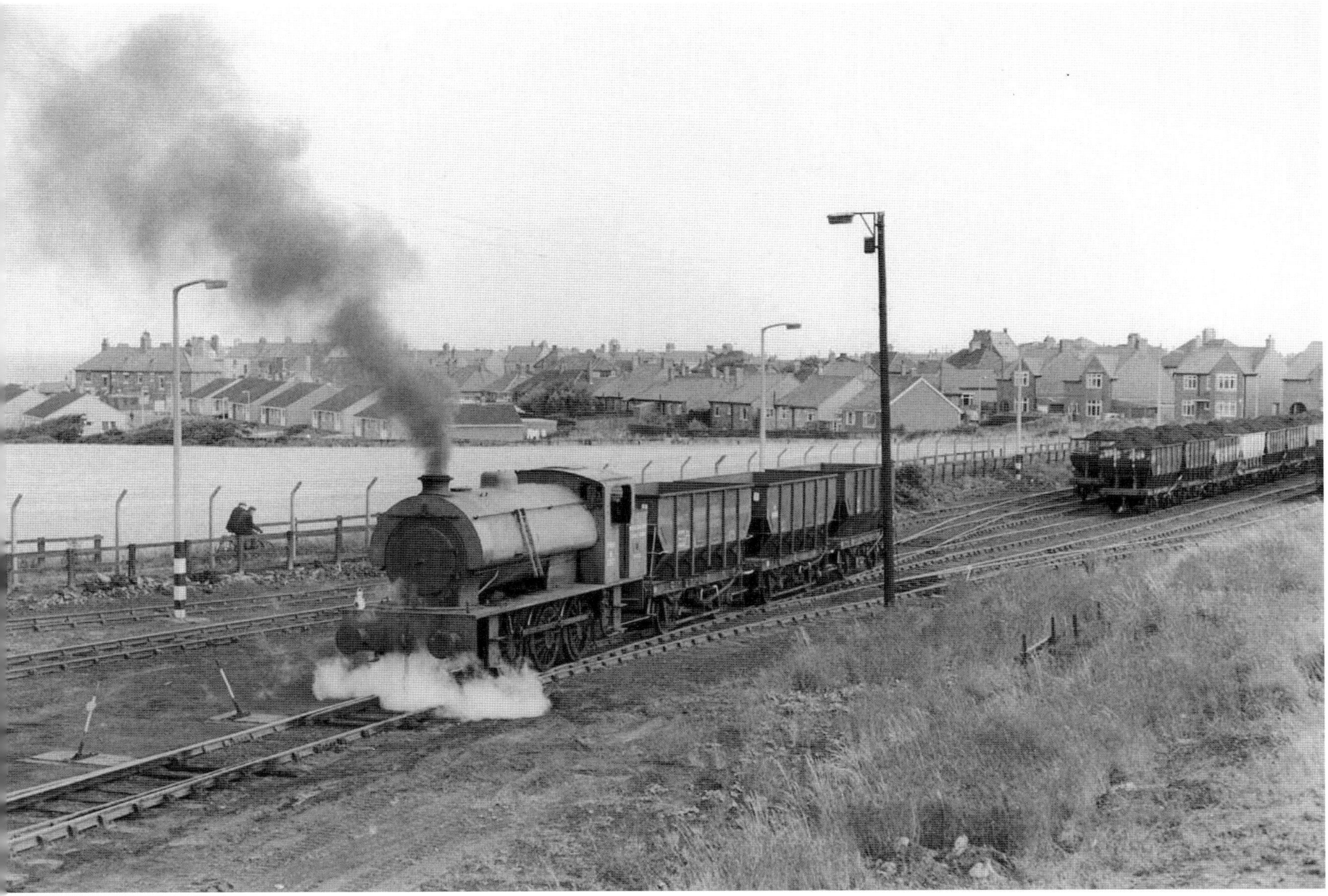

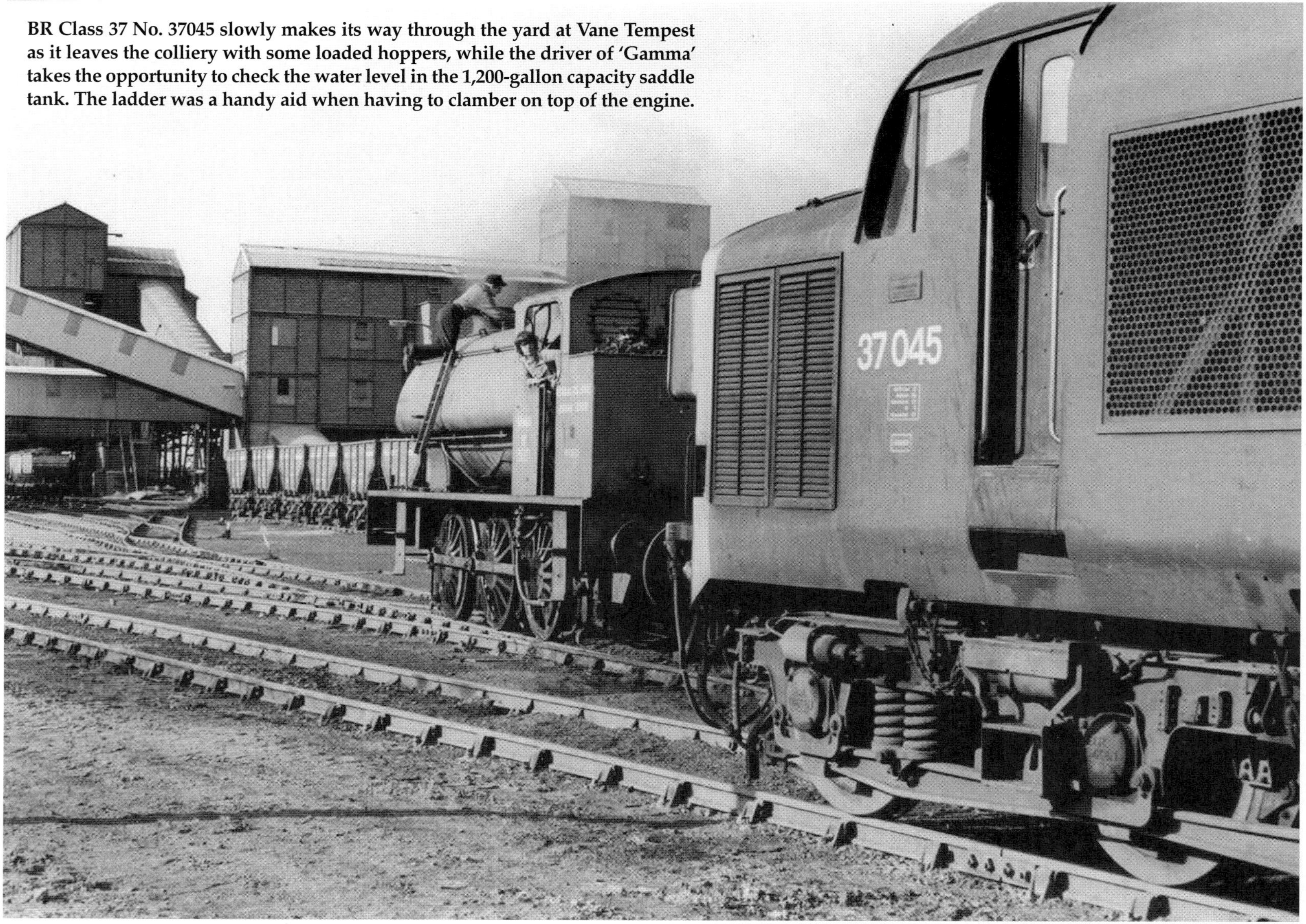

BR Class 37 No. 37045 slowly makes its way through the yard at Vane Tempest as it leaves the colliery with some loaded hoppers, while the driver of 'Gamma' takes the opportunity to check the water level in the 1,200-gallon capacity saddle tank. The ladder was a handy aid when having to clamber on top of the engine.

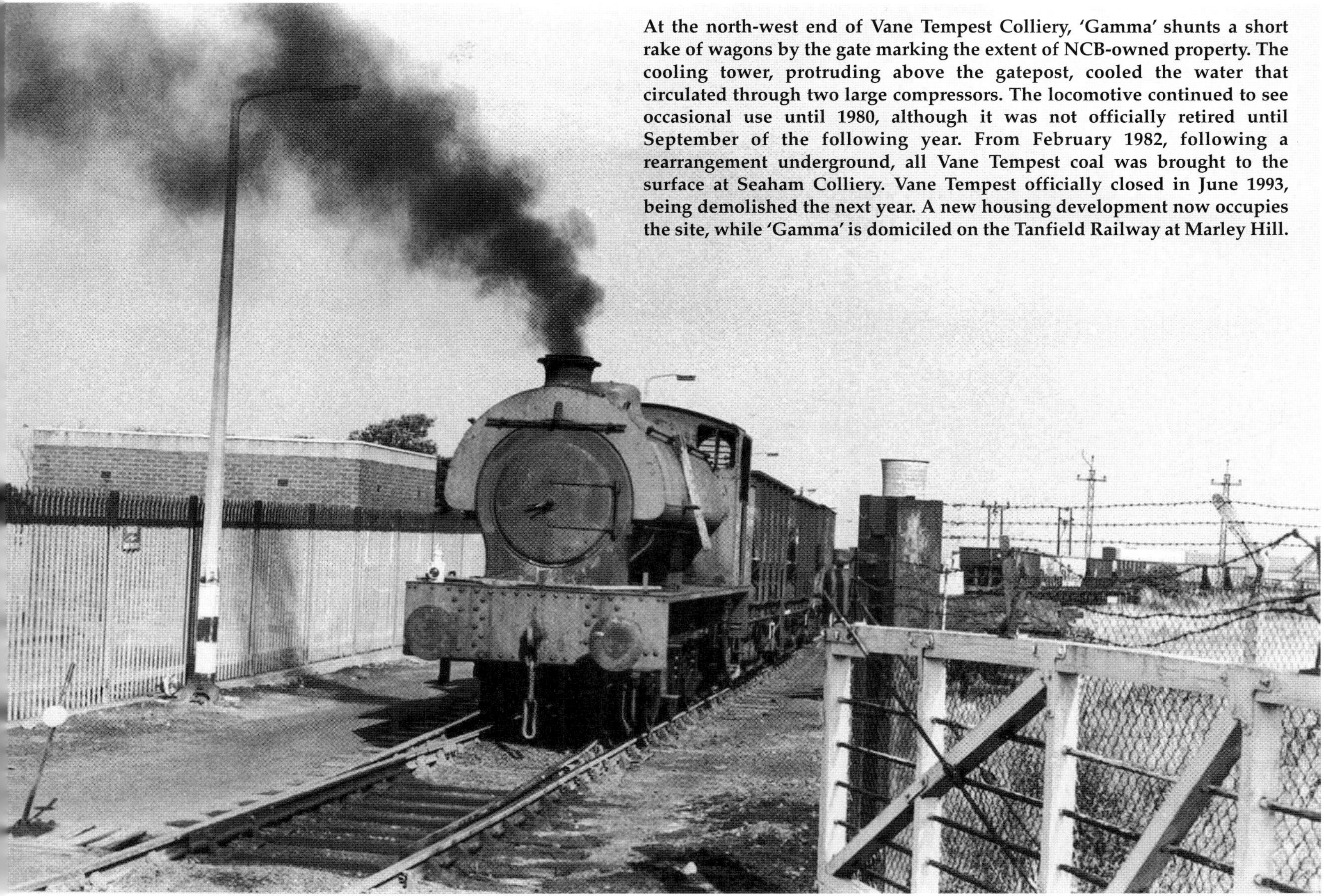

At the north-west end of Vane Tempest Colliery, 'Gamma' shunts a short rake of wagons by the gate marking the extent of NCB-owned property. The cooling tower, protruding above the gatepost, cooled the water that circulated through two large compressors. The locomotive continued to see occasional use until 1980, although it was not officially retired until September of the following year. From February 1982, following a rearrangement underground, all Vane Tempest coal was brought to the surface at Seaham Colliery. Vane Tempest officially closed in June 1993, being demolished the next year. A new housing development now occupies the site, while 'Gamma' is domiciled on the Tanfield Railway at Marley Hill.

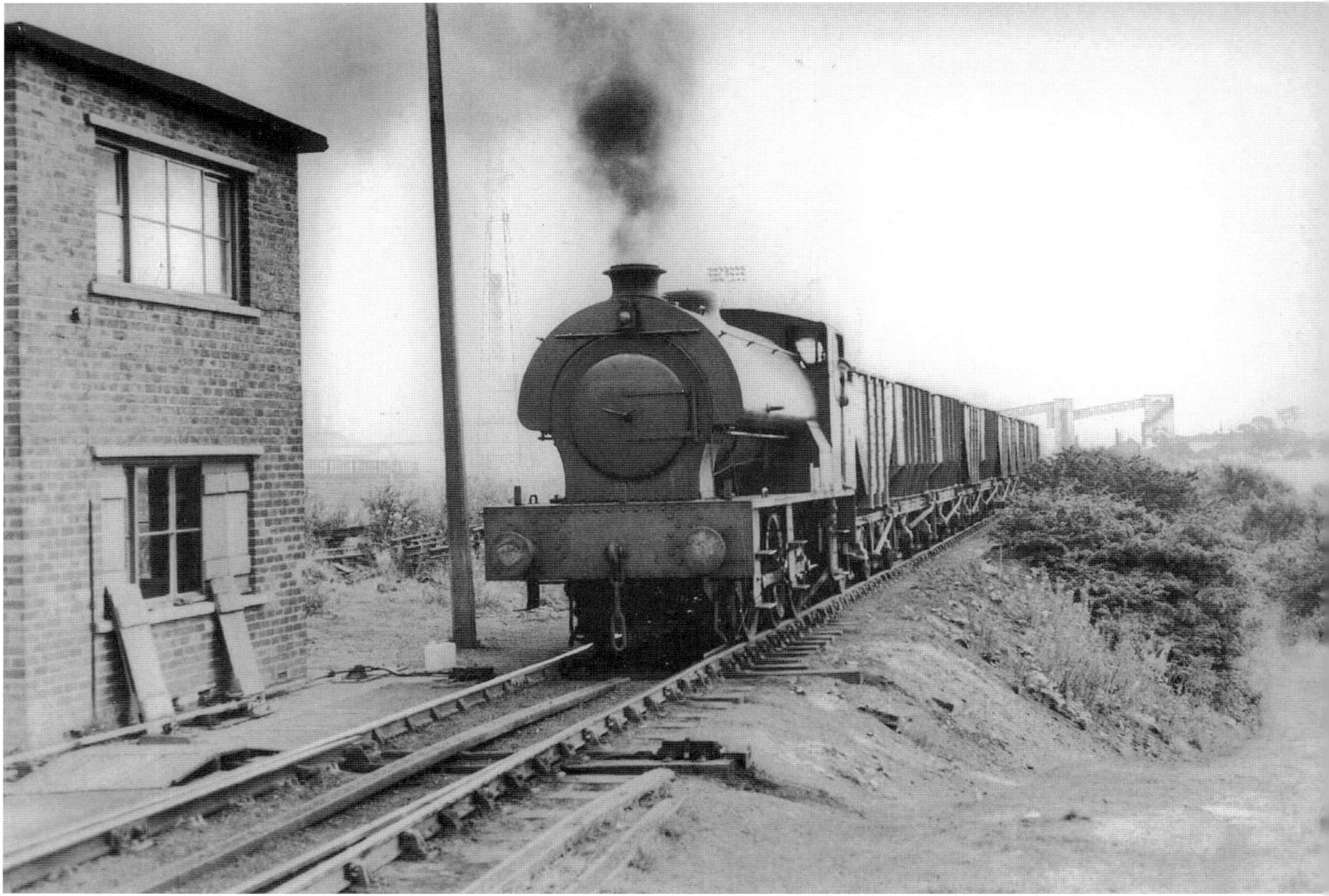

Opposite: The South Hetton Colliery Railway had a history dating back to the 1830s. Initially it linked the colliery of the same name to Seaham Harbour, some four miles distant, making use of two rope-worked inclines at its eastern extremity (see pages 42 and 43). In later years various extensions were built in order to serve other local collieries. During the early 1950s the NCB invested in a vast new mining complex at Hawthorn, to the south of Murton, in order to raise the coal produced by Elemore, Eppleton and Murton collieries at a central point, the new arrangements coming on stream from the end of 1959. The old collieries, however, retained their separate identities, although they were then used only as access points for men and materials. A new coking plant, erected at the same time, was fed by conveyor belts direct from the Hawthorn screens, the fifty W.D. Becker ovens being able to handle up to 390,000 tons of coal per annum, with the by-products of tar, rectified benzene, concentrated ammonia and gas for town use also being manufactured. To serve the development an extensive array of sidings were put down, with colour-light signals installed to assist the safe and efficient movement of trains. The scale of the operation can be gauged by the fact that during the year ending 31 December 1962, from a combined workforce of 4,702 men, a total of 1,484,978 tons of coal was lifted up the Hawthorn shafts. Here, with the Hawthorn complex in the background and ten wagons coupled behind, Hunslet 'Austerity' 0-6-0ST works No. 3687, NCB No. 62, approaches the signal control cabin on 30 August 1972. The engine was delivered direct to South Hetton (where the steam locomotives continued to be based) from the maker's factory in Leeds in January 1949.

Right: A few seconds later, looking in the opposite direction to the previous photograph, No. 62 makes its way towards South Hetton Colliery, which despite its proximity to the Hawthorn mine remained independent. In 1962 production totalled 281,191 tons, with 649 men working underground and a further 208 on the surface. Next to the locomotive is a NCB seven-plank hopper wagon designated for internal use only.

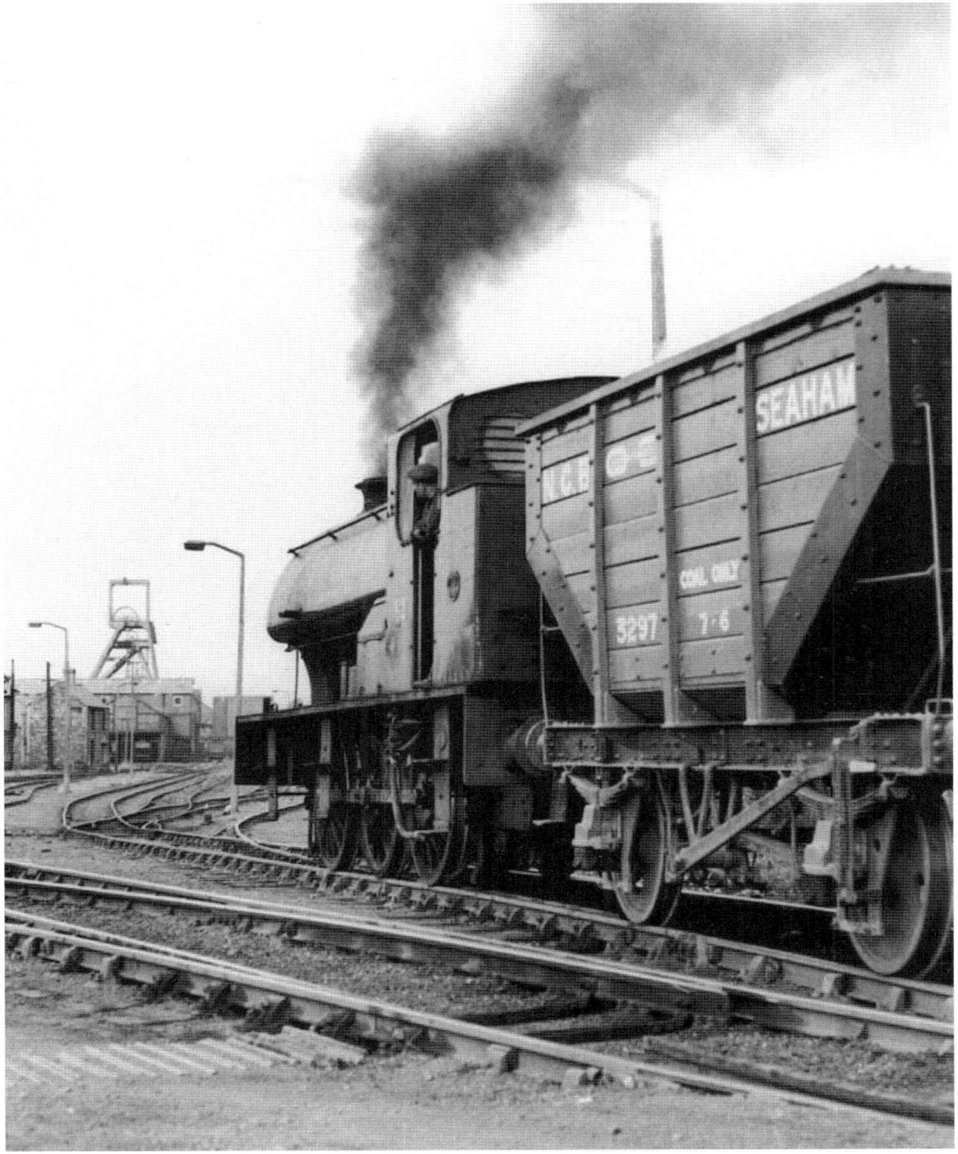

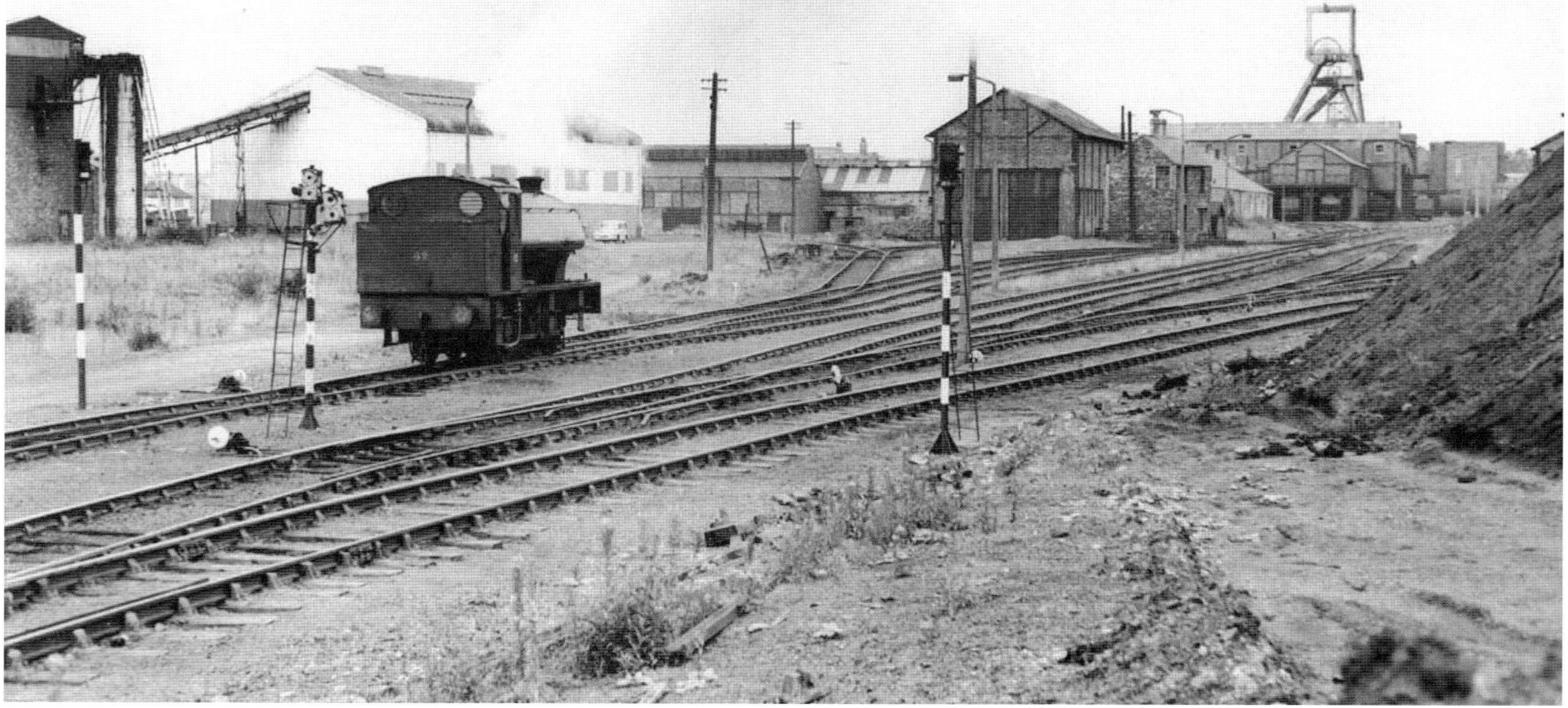

On the same day as the previous two photographs, No. 62 runs light engine through the yard at South Hetton Colliery. Some of the older buildings here contrasted sharply with the more modern structures at nearby Hawthorn. Notice too the colour-light signals. These were activated from the signal box seen on page 38. For many years six 'Austerities' were allocated to the shed at South Hetton, two built by Vulcan Foundry at Newton-le-Willows, Lancashire, in 1945, which had been handed down to the NCB by the South Hetton Coal Co. Ltd in 1947. The other four were purchased new by the NCB from the Hunslet Engine Company between 1949 and 1954. The sextet spent all their commercial working days at South Hetton; No. 62 was the last to be used, in the summer of 1976.

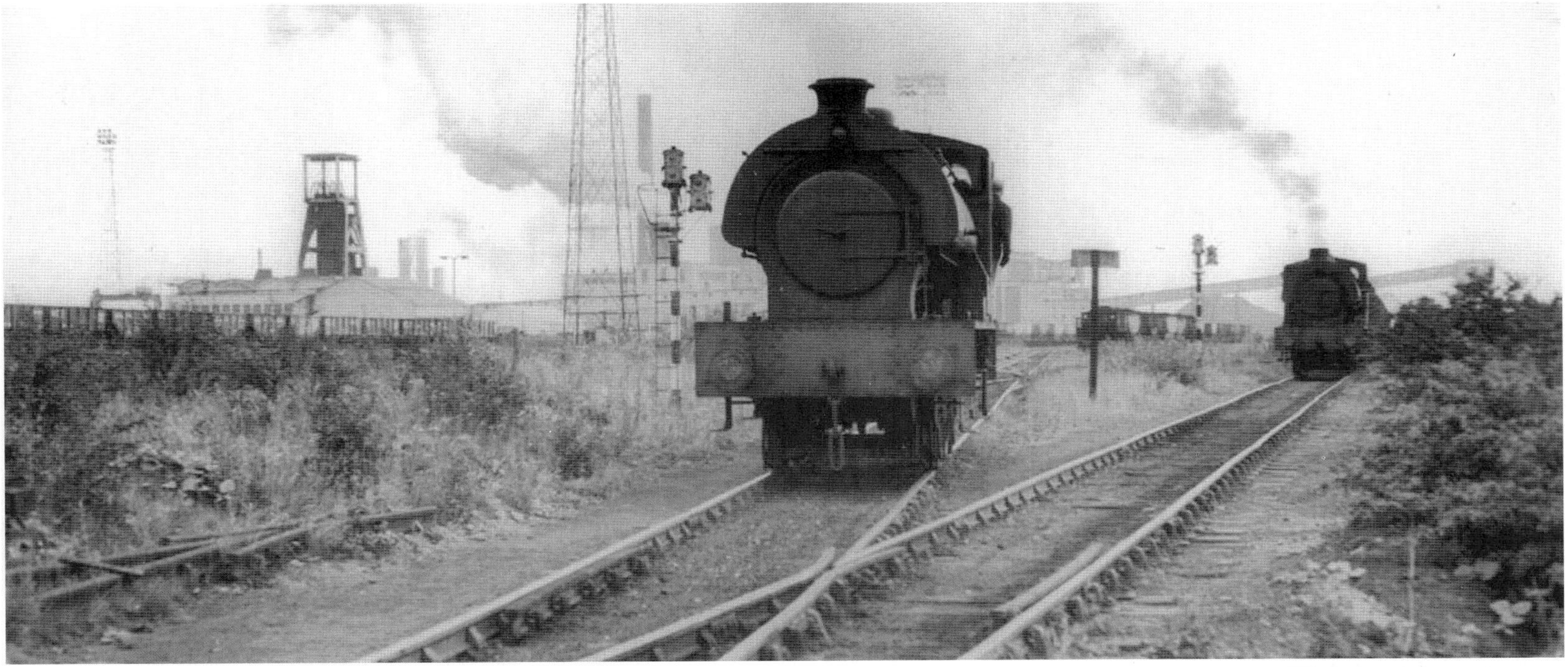

Above: Again on 30 August 1972, No. 62 reverses towards Hawthorn, as sister 'Austerity', NCB No. 69, built in 1953 as Hunslet works No. 3785, waits for the road with a string of empties from Seaham Harbour.

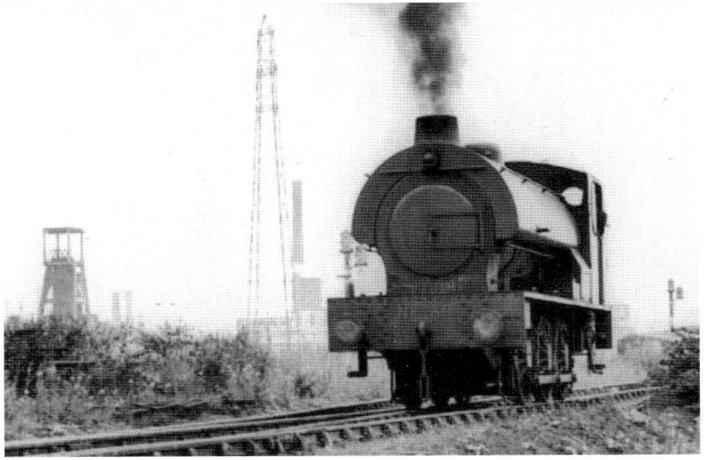

Right: A close-up view of No. 69. Prominent is the conical-shaped chimney fitted in 1964 when the locomotive was rebuilt with a Hunslet patent underfeed stoker and gas producer system, which was designed to reduce the amount of black smoke emitted. The last coal from the Hawthorn mine was wound in November 1991, the coking plant having already finished as production never restarted after the 1984/85 miners' strike. Two of the six 'Austerities' based here are still extant, No. 69 at the Embsay & Bolton Abbey Railway, near Skipton, North Yorkshire, and No. 72 (illustrated on the inside front cover) at the Llangollen Railway in North Wales. Regrettably, the other four were all scrapped.

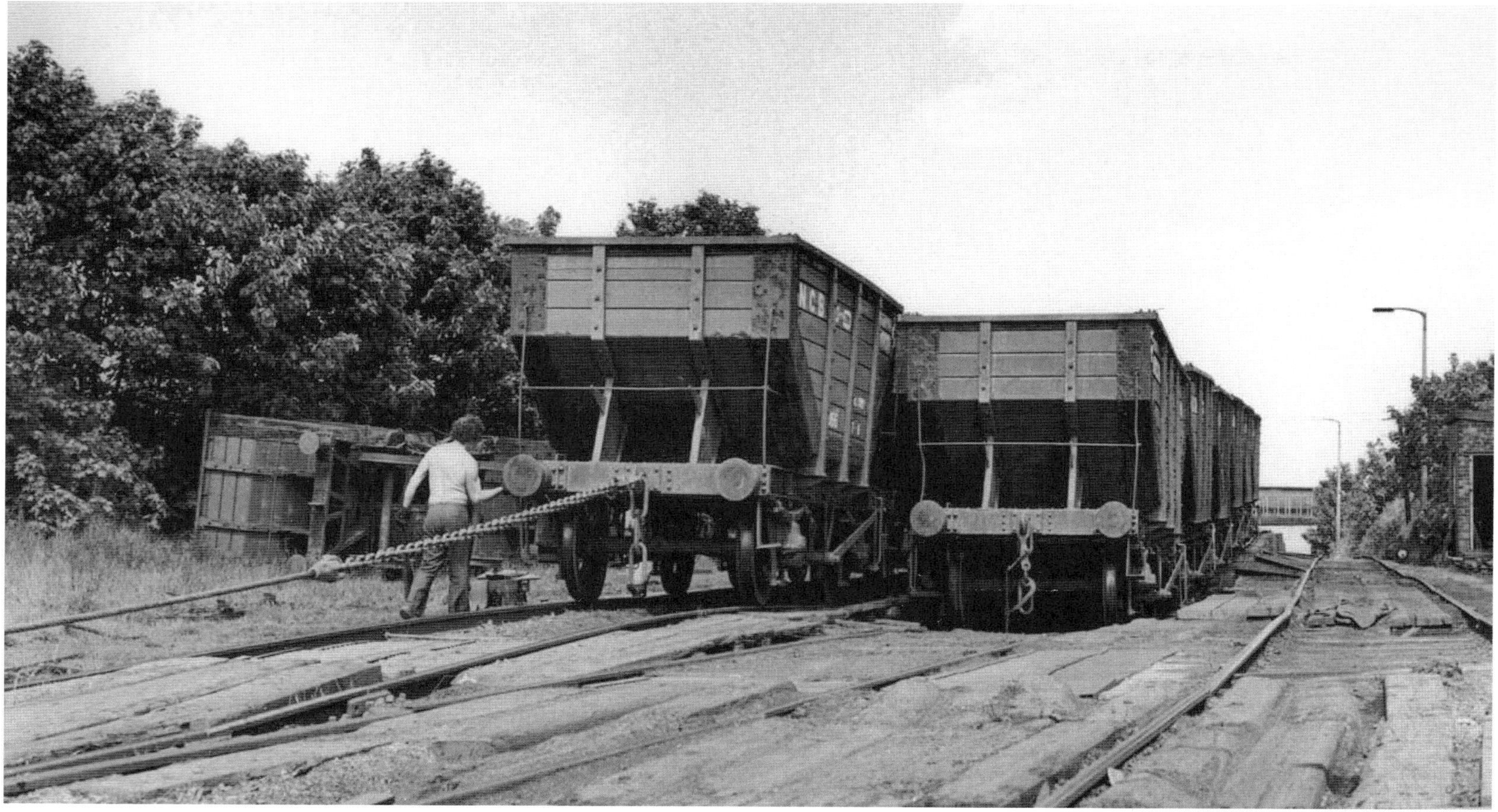

The collieries in the South Hetton area were located at a much higher altitude than the harbour at Seaham and, in order to access the latter, two self-acting inclines, in total one-and-a-half miles long, were engineered. The procedure at the foot of each section was for a set of six empty wagons to be attached to a rope which was wound round a drum at the top of the bank, and where the other end was hooked-up to a similar set of loaded wagons. Once the appropriate signals had been exchanged between the operatives and the brakes released, then gravity took over, the additional weight of the fulls on the downward run having enough force to hoist the empties up the steep gradient in the opposite direction, the two sets passing each other at the midway point. On the sunny afternoon of 5 June 1981 at Swine Lodge, where the two inclines met, the top section haulage rope is about to be released from the rear wagon of a descending set, before being fastened to some empties standing on the centre road, in preparation for the next stage of their journey to the summit at Hesledon Bank Top. At Swine Lodge the ascending wagons always passed along the centre 'kip' road, while those going down the gradient used the left and right-hand tracks alternately. To the left, an overturned hopper wagon from an earlier mishap lies derelict.

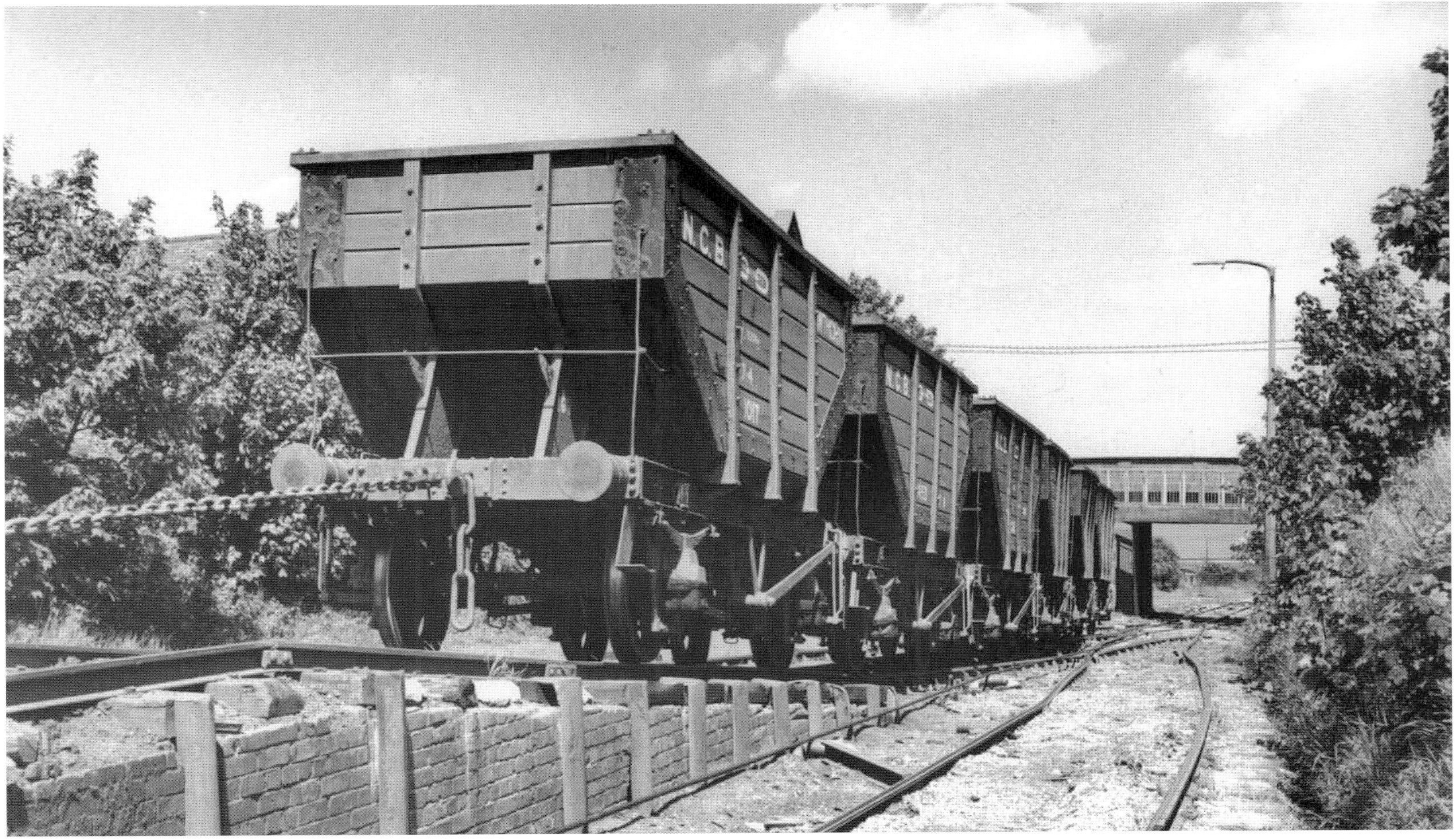

Later the same day at Swine Lodge the taut rope (with chain links attached for hooking up to the end wagon) drags a set of empties onto the 'kip', the momentum of the loaded wagons approaching the harbour being sufficient to lift them over the hump. They would then judder to a halt, the design preventing them from rolling backwards. Looking down the bank, under the bridge, the BR Sunderland to Hartlepool coast line can be seen crossing over the NCB tracks. Seaham Harbour lies beyond. By this time the inclines were no longer conveying coal for shipment elsewhere as in former years; instead they were used solely as a means of delivering waste material from South Hetton and Hawthorn to the harbour for dumping at sea. These were the last NCB self-acting inclines to remain in daily use, the 1984/85 miners' strike spelling the end. The trackbed of the inclines is now used as a footpath. Two similar inclines have been conserved by the Bowes Railway at Springwell, near Gateshead.

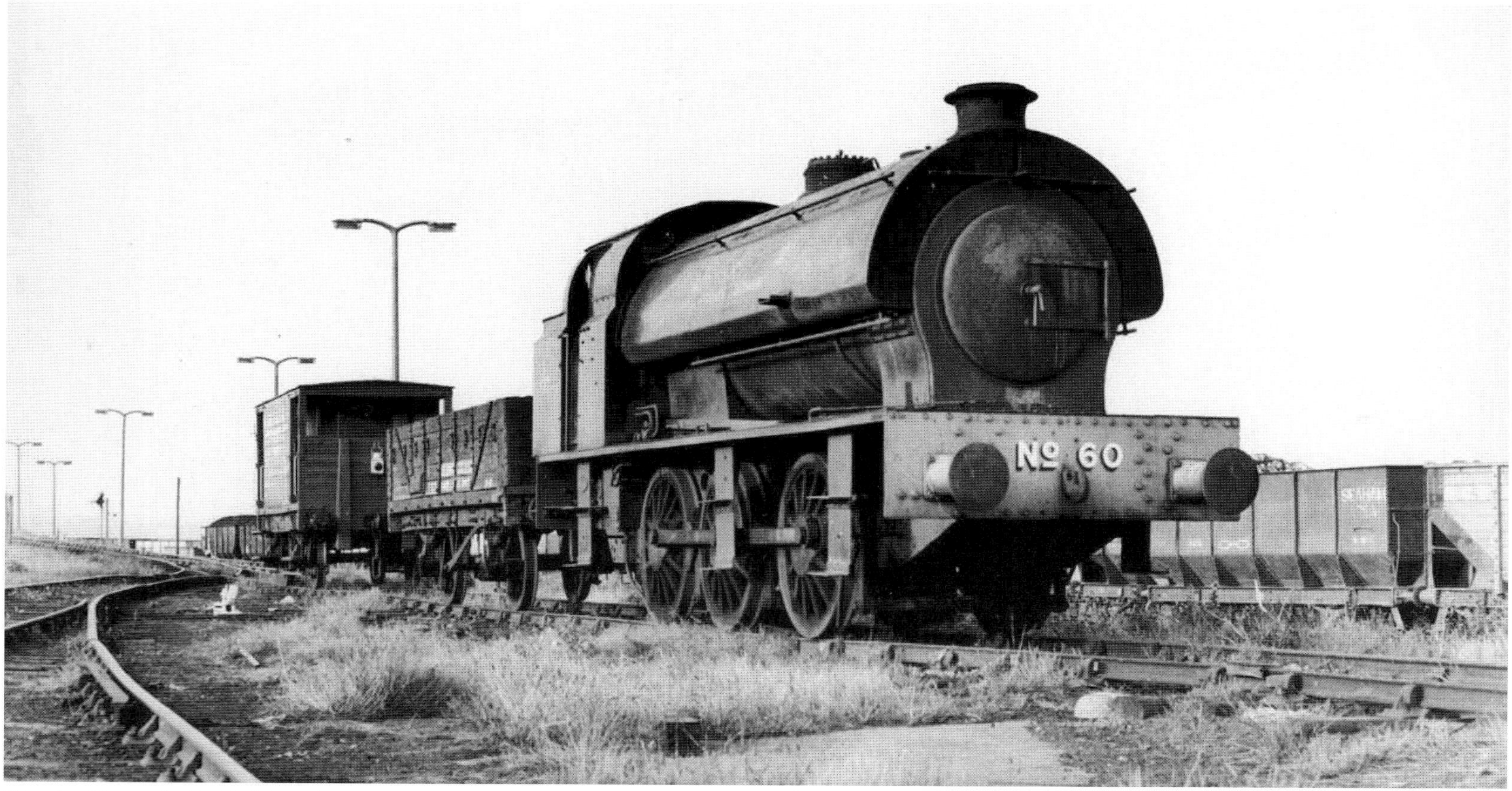

Hunslet 'Austerity' 0-6-0ST works No. 3686, NCB No. 60, bought fresh by the NCB in January 1949, stands dormant and minus its dome cover at Dawdon Colliery, just south of Seaham Harbour, on 28 August 1974. The engine had been allocated here since July 1965. The distinctive rounded cab profile was a throwback to its earlier days on the Lambton Railway, the adaptation being necessary so that it could pass through the narrow confines of Deptford Tunnel in order to access the staithes on the River Wear at Sunderland. The five-plank open wagon No. 132 was clearly marked 'Loco Coal Only', and was often left attached to the engine when shunting. Similarly, brake van No. 7 was also for internal use only. Dawdon was another colliery sunk by Londonderry Collieries Ltd, coal first being drawn in October 1907. It was a massive undertaking for within three years over 3,000 men had been engaged by the owners with approximately 1,000,000 tons of coal being excavated by hand annually. The colliery became fully mechanised in 1962 at a cost of £4 million, and in the early 1970s some 2,200 men were responsible for an annual output of approx 1,500,000 tons. All came to an end in July 1991 when the pit was closed. As regards No. 60, this is now on the stocklist of the Strathspey Railway at Aviemore in Scotland, while the brake van is on the Tanfield Railway at Marley Hill.

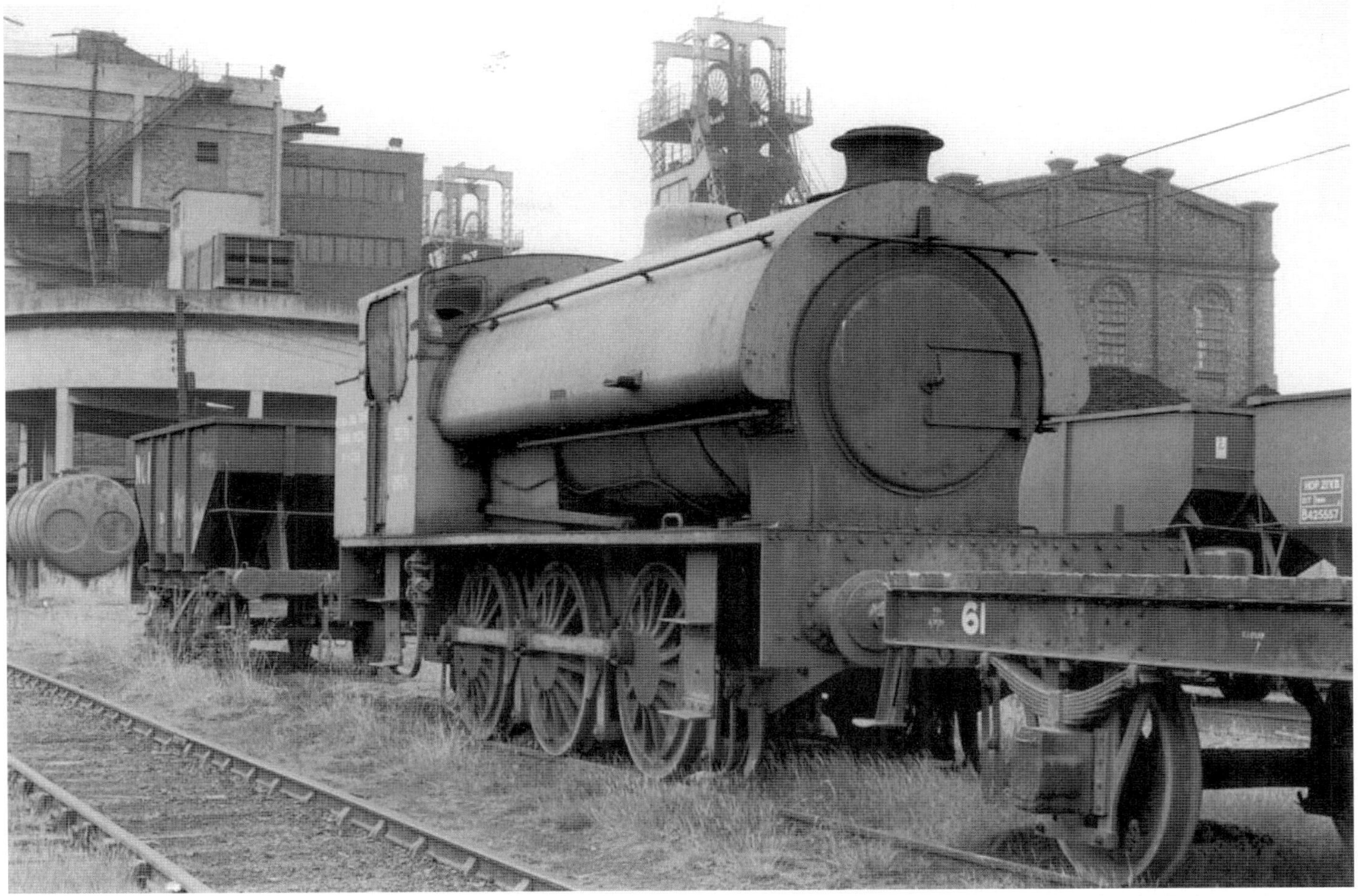

The next day, five miles south of Dawdon at Blackhall Colliery, Blackhall, another 'Austerity' 0-6-0ST, NCB No. 2502/11 'Delta', sporting a conventional style cab, was photographed against a backcloth of the colliery buildings. Assembled in October 1944 by the Hunslet Engine Company as works No. 3189, WD No. 75138, the locomotive was loaned to the Ministry of Fuel & Power and subsequently worked at a number of opencast sites in Northumberland. It became part of the assets of the NCB Opencast Executive when this was formed in April 1952. After a six-month sojourn in Derbyshire from September 1957, it returned north, this time to County Durham, eventually moving to Blackhall in September 1968. 'Delta' remained on the inventory there until it faced the breakers' hammers in August 1975. The colliery, after producing coal since 1913, ceased winding in January 1977 when it was connected underground to Horden Colliery.

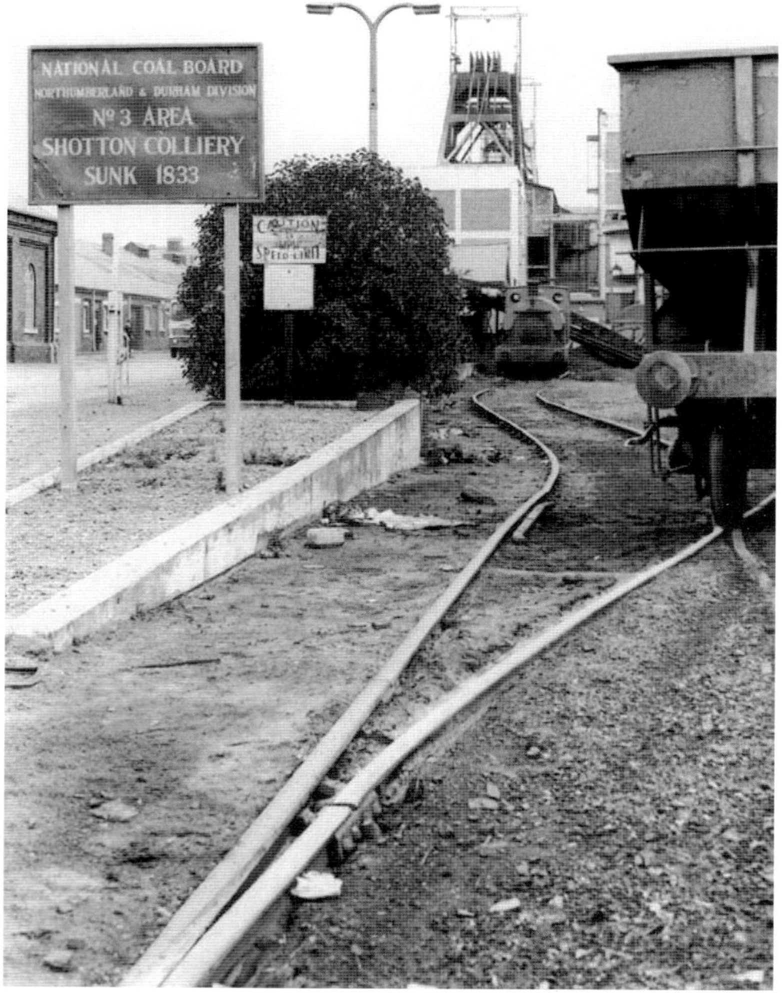

Like a number of similar communities in County Durham that were established in the vicinity of the local pit, the village of Shotton Colliery, two miles west of Peterlee, had the suffix 'Colliery' as part of its official title. The notice board by the entrance to the colliery on 29 August 1972, the day all the photographs at Shotton were taken, proudly stated that it had been sunk in 1833, although some sources record a later date. Despite the sign's reference to the Northumberland & Durham Division of the NCB, formed on 1 January 1964, due to a further restructuring scheme the colliery had in fact been administered by the South Durham Area since the latter's creation on 26 March 1967. Under the shadow of the winding gear stands Peckett Class B2 0-6-0ST works No. 1310, which was supplied new by the Bristol-based company in May 1914 to Horden Collieries Ltd, the then owners of Shotton, as well as Blackhall and Horden collieries. It had 14in. diameter outside cylinders with a 20in. stroke and 3ft 7in. diameter wheels. The engine was dismantled for scrap the following November.

Over the years the colliery had had a chequered history. Initially known as Shotton Grange Colliery it was closed down in November 1877. However, it was back in production from 1901 under new owners, Horden Collieries Ltd, this company also reviving the fortunes of the associated brickworks and coking plant. In 1915 the coking plant's original beehive ovens were replaced by a battery of sixty Koppers regenerative ovens, these being capable of processing 166,000 tons of coal per annum, the by-products of tar, sulphate of ammonia, crude benzole and gas also being available for sale. The brickworks and the coking plant both ceased production during the late 1950s, the former having been sold off by the NCB in 1953. Thus, only the colliery remained at the time of the author's visit and, sadly, at the end of the same week, Friday 1 September 1972, this too was closed.

Opposite: A portrait of the working engine at Shotton during its last months, a rather decrepit looking Andrew Barclay 0-6-0ST, works No. 1015, built in 1904. Its identity was not readily apparent to the casual observer, the maker's identification plates having been removed from the cab side-sheets as evidenced by the resultant marks. The engine had 15in. x 22in. outside cylinders and 3ft 5in. diameter wheels. Like the Peckett locomotive based at Shotton (seen in the previous photograph), it had also been purchased new by Horden Collieries Ltd. Beyond the boundary wall can be seen part of a row of fifteen terraced houses on Farrow Street, a number of similar properties in the neighbourhood being equally convenient for the local miners. Since the closure of the colliery most of these terraces have been demolished and replaced by more modern housing stock.

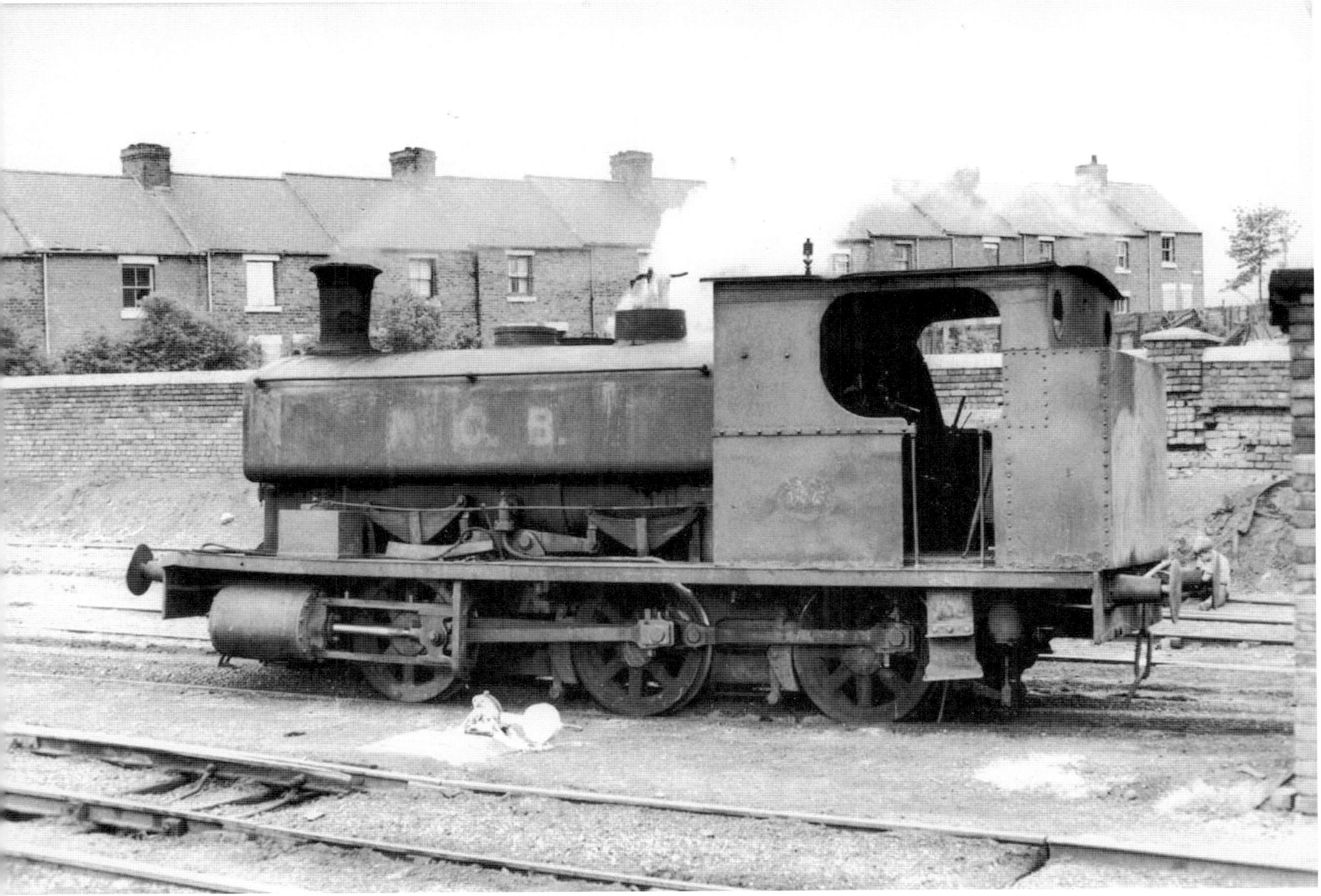
N.C.B.

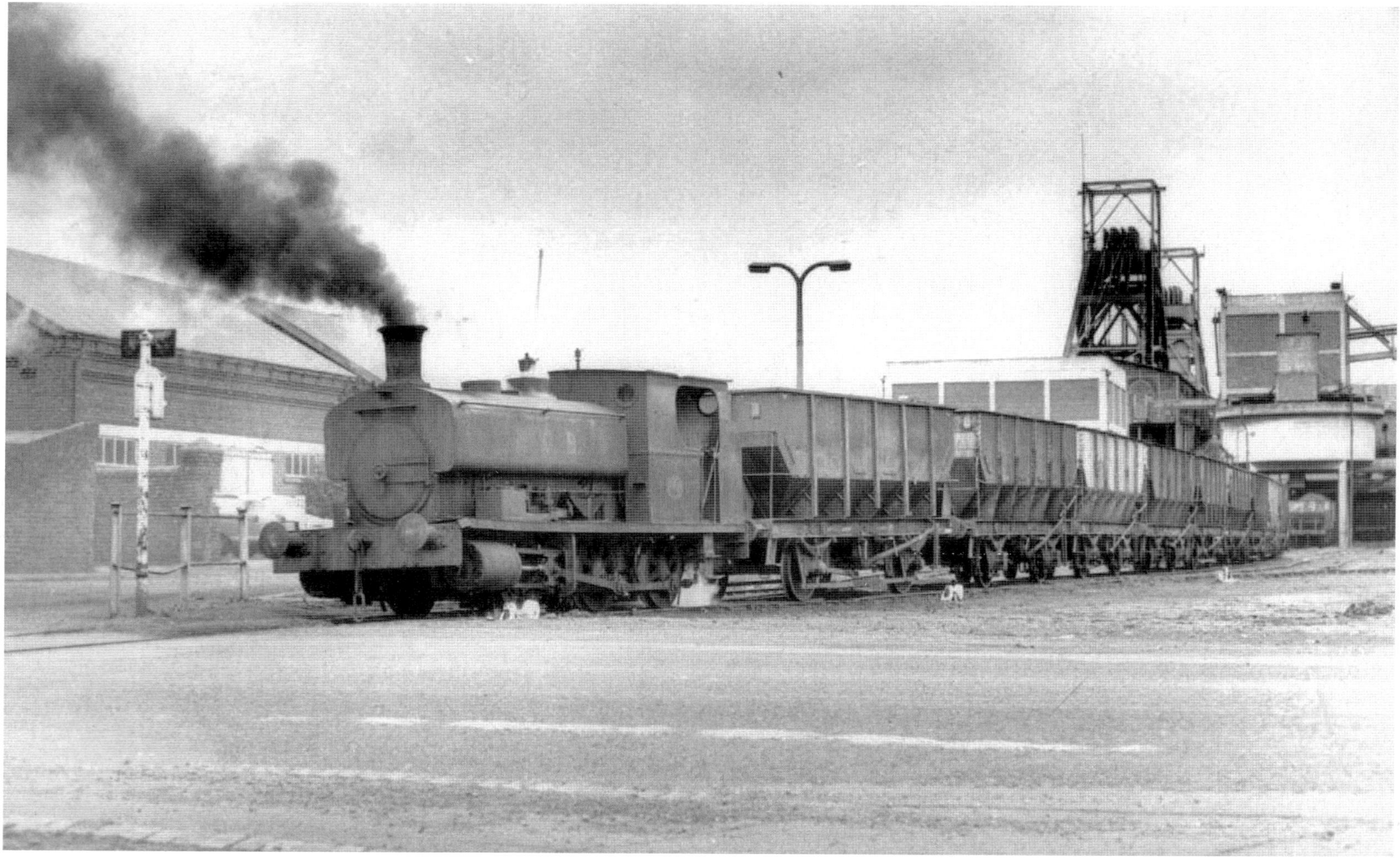

Here the Andrew Barclay 0-6-0ST propels nine empty hoppers towards the screens at Shotton ready for refilling. In 1947 the dominant winding wheels in the background daily lowered up to 1,350 men to their place of work underground, these having the support of a further 440 men on the surface. Their endeavours realised 488,800 tons of saleable coal for coking, gas and household purposes that year. By 1962 the number of men descending the shafts on a regular basis had been reduced to 815 and with the assistance of a further 251 who were employed above ground, 296,616 tons of coal was drawn over the weighbridge during the course of the year.